I0707499

A New American Evolution
To Save Our World

Mark Landau

ALSO BY MARK LANDAU

End the Fight

The Miracle Revolution

What We Can Do

The Love and Forgiveness Meditation

I Love You and Forgive You:
A True Self-Healing Tool and the Life Around It

Archetypes, Election, Evolution:
America's Denial of Democracy

CONTENTS

To Whistleblowers and Evolutionaries Everywhere

1 ARMAGEDDON

We inhabit an amazing, precious world.

And we desecrate it.

We have amazing, precious lives.

And we desecrate them.

For five thousand years, we have lived the path of greed and dominance.

This has been the inner force driving the power core of our human race.

It has taken us far, as far as it can.

But it has passed the point of diminishing returns.

It has all but destroyed our decency and quality of life.

It now threatens our planetary existence.

The potential for disaster and renewal is staggering.

We are at the crossroads of our existence.

Which way will we choose?

There are so many wonderful people doing the best they can for themselves, their loved ones and the world, being considerate, being responsible, taking care to live gently and rightly on planet Earth.

But this no longer is enough.

We hurtle towards self-destruction, lemmings to the sea, relentlessly driven by the lust for power and profit.

And there is so much frailty, fallibility and woundedness.

So many who have relinquished responsibility.

We dwell on dissing our leaders but do little, ourselves, to save our world.

What can one person do when such a great power block steers us towards malevolent destruction, when they hold the world's purse strings and policies like the reins of a mighty team?

Quite a lot.

I wish to speak to us all, the collective, the best and the worst in us, as if we were one.

I wish to lay bare our condition, to paint a picture in a different light and then do so much more.

I wish to rant, exhort, expand comprehension and reveal a way forward.

Much may seem harsh, but all is at stake and someone must.

Fasten your seatbelt.

There's something coming.

Take this bumpy ride with me.

We are all responsible.

Our potential future is far more promising than we can see.

And it needs you.

We know we're in trouble, do we not?

Our legal, financial and political systems are corrupt to the bone.

We have enshrined legalized crime.

We have deified corporations and enslaved ourselves to them.

We have sold our souls to money.

Our fine line of presidents, congressmen and justices should be ashamed of themselves.

Those who continue to rape our planet should be ashamed of themselves.

We who drug, drink and entertain ourselves to death should be ashamed of ourselves.

Let us feel our shame, if only for a moment.

We may not be the perpetrators, but we all have allowed it to happen, through our ignorance, complacency and passivity.

We are Nero fiddling while Rome burns.

But it has also simply come about, willy nilly, with or without us.

And it needed to come to this, this free fall, this breakdown of everything, this cracking and crumbling of the entire infrastructure of our past world edifice.

We must acknowledge and embrace the corruption with which we have poisoned our world.

We know it sickens us.

But now we must do something about it.

We treat the world as something to grab and steal from.

We treat each other as hits.

We adore and empower those who steal from and despise us.

We avoid and deny what we do to Mother Earth.

It is time to wake up.

It is time to face the truth.

It is time to enact massive, radical reform on every level of our society.

It is time for us to take back our world.

Our current course will undo us.

Our only choice is to make a great leap.

This leap must occur both within us, in our hearts, souls and psyches, and in the mechanisms that rule our world.

We must come to new laws, behaviors, policies and understandings.

We must rethink our world.

We have it within us to create a truly wonderful existence or to all go down together, despairing, fighting and dying.

Man-made climate disruption is real. Anyone who denies it is short-sighted, self-serving, ignorant and malignant. Our carbon dioxide count is higher than it's been for millions of years. And it's risen far more precipitously than it ever has.

Extreme weather has become so obvious as to be undeniable.

To ignore it is catastrophe.

To continue ignoring it is mass extinction.

Billions of dollars have been wasted in denying it.

We have seen this behavior before.

The super-wealthy tobacco industry denied that tobacco was addictive while they added chemicals to make it more so. And they funded a disinformation campaign to deny that habitually inhaling smoke into one's lungs caused cancer.

The fossil fuel industry is far wealthier than the tobacco industry was.

They continue to buy politicians and media icons to deny what we do to our only home.

We still have time, but barely.

Enough of us, together, can turn this world around, not only ecologically, but morally, economically and societally, as well.

We are within a hair's breadth of nuclear terrorism or war.

On January 25, 2018, the Bulletin of the Atomic Scientists advanced their Doomsday Clock to two minutes to midnight, the closest it's ever been, only equaled in 1953 at the height of the cold war.

We must turn this around, as well.

Nothing short of a great human leap will do.

I have been calling it The Miracle Revolution because, if we manage it, it will engender miracles.

Sixty Canadians got together in May of 2015 and decided to call it The Leap.

They created a party-less platform, The Leap Manifesto.

It contains the directions in which we must go.

There has already been progress.

Denmark and Germany are proving that parts of it can work.

A few Native and other Americans have begun the process, as well.

It's beginning to spread.

This can benefit everyone.

It is one of a number of new, brilliant advances and avenues of endeavor highlighted throughout this book that truly have the potential to turn our world around.

Read Naomi Klein's *No Is Not Enough* for a good understanding of where we are, how we got here and The Leap Manifesto.

Continue reading this book for these critical developments and a deeper understanding and appreciation of our truest, most profound potential.

Read my *End the Fight* and *What We Can Do* for what must occur within enough of us to support the real transformation these new evolving programs could spark.

Take them to heart. Put into practice what we literally must do to survive.

Get on board.

We must supercharge true, fundamental, benevolent change.

The lies and tweaks of the old, corrupt, thieving order will lead us to oblivion. The roots of corruption run deep.

Our way of living has become a tree of death. It must be uprooted and replaced with the tree of life.

This can be done beautifully, even smoothly, though the worst of the entrenched plutocracy will threaten Armageddon and, perhaps, assassinate a few of us along the way.

But who knows, perhaps some of them will actually see the light and come around.

We cannot wait for them.

We cannot wait for any savior.

We can and must come together to do this ourselves.

Ever since democracy was conceived and implemented there has been a tug of war between it and the rich.

After all, if the majority rules, why don't they simply take the wealth of the few for themselves?

The rich and powerful have always oppressed, abused and stolen from the poor.

And, over the millennia, they have gotten better and better

at it.

They have used many modalities to transfer more wealth to themselves and keep the masses in line.

The more enlightened have advocated generosity, lifting the workers up and treating them well so they would be happy enough not to rebel.

These kinds of policies and organized labor led to a large, healthy middle class and well-paid workers in our own, earlier US history.

Others have advocated diminishing democracy and squeezing the workers.

This is what Alan Greenspan said we must do and further implemented.

So our healthy middle and decently living working classes have all but been destroyed.

According to Forbes and a 2011 Swiss Federal Institute of Technology study, 147 interlocking super corporations control 40% of global economic power. 737 control 80%. The top echelons of companies like Disney, Amazon and Walmart earn billions and the lowest live in tents and are malnourished.

And, of course, so many have to work two, three and four jobs just to survive.

It's despicable.

The corporate masters should be ashamed of themselves.

But, of course, they are not.

They're quite proud of their over-bloat and accomplishments.

They're on top of the world, screwing away for all they are worth, caring nothing for the hordes of menials they abuse, feeling perfectly entitled to get away with everything they can at the expense of those below and in the world.

The wealthy have devised ever more ingenious, arcane, 'legal' ways to steal from the masses nearly all the wealth there is.

It is time to redress this.

It is time for the masses to become intelligent enough to do something about it.

It is time for the people to win.

It is time for the truly benevolent to structure our economy and society in a new, better, more equitable way.

Such a thing is possible and must soon come about.

Together, we must make it happen.

Time is running out.

Mother Earth, if we stop destroying her and organize our society truly well, does have the resources to allow us all to live well and thrive.

If we shepherd and treat her well, she will reward us.

But we race to destroy her.

Our wealth and legacy have been stolen.

We have a false concept of ownership.

We strive to own nature.

Our agribusiness practices and monocrops deplete our soil and pollute our land and oceans.

The great criminals Monsanto, Syngenta and others strive to own the genetic codes of our natural world and contaminate every seed on Earth (watch *Seed: The Untold Story*).

The giant chemical companies race to poison our most sacred, precious places.

We have created a voracious, Monty Python corporatocracy completely blind to the protection of life and decency.

Our patriarchal way is to own, control and screw the planet and everyone we can.

Ever greater power and greed trampling everything in its path.

This is the self-destructing dinosaur we have become.

We have mistreated each other and our living world far too long.

Ever smaller numbers have amassed ever greater wealth and power.

This has been done through a great series of maneuvers that is strangling us and our environment.

As I edit this, our Senate has passed their new tax codes. Corker, the last Republican holdout, finally buckled when they added a new provision benefitting Real Estate Moguls, of which he and Trump are two.

This is a perfect example of how completely self-serving our legislators have become. These tax codes are neither popular nor good for our country. They hurt many more than they help. They are a formula for disaster.

But this doesn't matter. All that matters is that they enrich the legislators enacting them. It is a naked display of the height of our corruption and the natural extension of the wealthy amassing more wealth to themselves and stealing more from the rest of us.

They know full well the result will be a dramatic increase to our national deficit. This is their plan. It will then be their excuse to cut funding for Social Security, Medicare, Medicaid and other parts of the safety net that supports the survival of so many of us, 'entitlements' that we have paid for and are truly entitled to. They wish to steal that money, as well. They are already preparing us to swallow this.

The April 9, 2018, edition of the New York Times quoted Keith Hall, director of the Congressional Budget Office, regarding the projection that the federal budget deficit will soar to over $1 Trillion in 2020.

"The longer you wait the more draconian the measures have to be to fix the problem."

This is how they massage us into submission.

And in ending net neutrality they have succeeded in their favorite ploy, rigging the rules to transform the Internet from the free, egalitarian font of information and service it has been to benefit the mighty few.

We might hope that, in these things, we have reached the height of our dysfunction.

But we can't only hope.

We must begin to do everything we can to make sure it is.

We could make these the final convulsions of our business as usual greed machine.

Or we could let it continue to our destruction.

We must see all this clearly and rise to the occasion.

Let this solstice day mark our darkest hour.

It could, you know.

We could make it so.

On the flip side of current events, the MeToo/TimesUp Movement has shown what can happen when the oppressed stand up and speak out against the abusive powerful.

These brave women have shown how easily the titans can topple when the masses confront them.

Perhaps in some cases there's been overcompensation, but in most cases, not. And it's been telling, empowering, long overdue and will ultimately be unifying.

The lessons are coming thicker and faster, more and more grandiosely and more and more in our face.

Will we see what's before our eyes?

Will we learn the lessons that bombard us?

We can and must begin to dismantle our corrupt system, restructure our tax codes for the benefit of all, retrieve stolen wealth, gut and rewrite many of our current laws, reclaim what truly belongs to all of us and redress the imbalance.

We must build local, life-supporting, democratically owned energy and agricultural farms and adopt the evolving policies of The Leap Manifesto.

We can and must demand and reclaim our decency, freedom, respect and right behavior on every level of our society.

But, in order to do this, we must reawaken within.

We must get our house, heart and head in order.

We must realize what we are capable of.

We must remember who we truly are.

2 RECLAMATION

It's clearly possible to structure society in a way that is beneficial to all.

There have been national and cultural pockets that have approached this to the greater benefit of the larger numbers.

After World War II was such a time in America.

But it, also, to a large degree, was based on theft—feeding the war machine through invasion after invasion and plundering the resources of those countries and others.

We live in a different world.

But we could do better than we ever have.

The only thing lacking is the will and intelligence of the masses.

The masses are easily duped.

They are misled, brainwashed, de-educated and manipulated through PR and a corrupt media.

They are distracted by shock politics and histrionics.

They lionize the worst of us.

But sooner or later, even the reddest of necks will begin to catch on, won't they?

The thieves they are voting in are ripping them off.

We are deeply embedded in a vicious cycle.

The spinmeisters have spun the brains right out of us.

As many of us as possible must crystalize our

understanding and see through all the shit.

So, for a moment, let's dream and imagine what we might do to leap out of this quagmire.

No regulation leads to runaway greed.

The pharmaceuticals, the casino banks, the insurance companies, even the utilities will constantly push to gouge, steal and inflate their bottom lines to the detriment of everyone and everything.

As long as money is our God and nothing else matters, we are doomed.

There are things more important than money.

True morality, ethics and decency trump money.

Safeguarding what is truly precious trumps money.

Honesty trumps money, though obviously, not in our current politics nor in our current mass psyche.

But at the deepest levels of our souls, hearts and spirits, it does.

In our highest knowing.

At the core of our being.

In our lost wisdom.

It appears as if we have lost our wisdom, our common sense, the difference between truth and falsehood, right and wrong.

But we haven't.

It's still there, deep within us.

It is time to re-find and reclaim it.

Doing the inner work can help.

Meditation can help.

But in the world at large, we must find a balance that works better for us all.

Are we beginning to realize this?

We have made corporations super people, with more rights than humans.

But they are not people.

They only recognize profit.

So they must be regulated, including the amounts they can shower on their corrupt CEOs.

Sensible caps can be put in place.

Significant portions of the money stolen from shareholders can be retrieved.

Funds stolen from taxpayers to bail out criminal financial institutions can also be retrieved.

The shuffling and gambling of capital paper must be regulated.

Commercial and speculative banks should be completely separated, so those who utilize the services of the former can have the trust that their bank won't be engaged in the riskier practices of the latter.

A true, state central bank owned by the people and run by a board of honest, unvested, economic minds should replace the privately owned Federal Reserve system in setting interest rates and printing money, the act of which should in no way incur debt.

All Federal Reserve assets should be frozen and returned to the public coffers. Those private institutions have stolen from us long enough.

Workable, common sense laws can be formulated to harness the various business sectors, so they can still perform well without wildly stampeding to the detriment of the rest of us.

I have already mentioned our corrupt tax codes.

More and more they benefit the super wealthy and squeeze everyone else.

They must not be allowed to stand.

The super wealthy have had their way with us for long enough.

It is time we rise up to reclaim what has been stolen and, in intelligent ways, to set things right.

We must change the rules of the game so that no individual institution or individual can gain super wealth and super power.

We can redress the imbalance with tax codes without loopholes that tax the wealthy and all corporations in sensible, workable ways without crippling or bankrupting them but tempering their bloat to within sane limits.

Transaction taxes can fund a healthy, more renewable infrastructure and a far better public transport system.

We can remove many of the restrictive regulations strangling small business and place necessary regulations on big business.

We must change the rules of the money game so that it becomes a fairer, more equitable game.

Our healthcare system, with its obscene profits for the pharmaceutical and insurance companies, is a titanic, wasteful travesty. It steals from all of us and drains our national health and wealth. It can be totally and judiciously revamped.

Polluters, especially, should pay. We need carbon and chemical pollution taxes. Speculative gain should also be the most highly taxed.

Instead, we have been letting the worst of us get away with the most.

The solutions are out there. They can be found and implemented to eliminate our corrupt laws, to heal our sickening justice system.

Laws can be reformed and rewritten.

Prisons for profit are obscene.

Decades long jail terms for non-violent crimes are revolting.

Criminalizing drug use and prostitution has never and will never work.

These things can be regulated in ways that don't feed our corruption.

All of this rot can be flushed out of the system.

The ultra-conservatives are right. The swamp must be drained. But not according to their lights. They are responsible for much of it.

We can set things right if enough of us find our will.

"It'll never happen," most might say.

But it must if we are to survive.

We are facing things that man has never faced.

One way or another, massive change will force itself upon

us.

> Defeatism won't do.
> We can fix this.
> Will we find the intelligence and will to do so?

3 EVOLUTION

Life evolves in seemingly eternal phases of foundation building then in great leaps of faster, profound progress.

For the longest time, single-celled organisms proliferated in the oceans till they became a nearly full soup of them. Then, one fine day, cells started combining and the race was on. This continued for eons while the land, regarding animal life, mostly lay fallow. Then another great leap took place in the form of centipede-like ocean critters and then certain fish crawling out of the sea. This led to a great spurt in land evolution.

Human evolution goes much more quickly but, from our perspective, seems to drag on forever or even stop.

But it doesn't.

It follows the chakras, our major energy centers strung out along our spines, each with its own dominant qualities, natures and wisdom.

Our first stage was the hunter-gatherer.

This was the root chakra age, ruled by the energy center just above the perineum, a rudimentary, masculine one revolving around survival, tribe, sign, symbol and magic and the oneness of things.

Then came the second, feminine chakra age with its first separation, wherein the human race began to distance itself from and partner with, harness and shepherd nature through agriculture and husbandry, the cultivation of crops, the care for and domestication of animals, the matriarchy, fertility, the goddess cults, myth and the impulses of sustenance, nurturing and the miracle of the seed and procreation.

This second chakra is located in the womb area, both men and women having the subtle energy organs of the opposite sex.

Then, around five thousand years ago, the shift to the diaphragm, masculine, third chakra functioning began with the second separation as we moved from partnering, worshipping and respecting nature to dominating and subjugating her and the patriarchal, Indo-Aryan and other invading conquerors begin sweeping the world to murder, rape and destroy the matriarchs of the previous age and grab and subdue everything in sight, treating people and nature as things, machines and objects of ownership and creating the world religions, the mode that has been ruling us ever since.

Make no mistake, women and the matriarchy suppressed and controlled men almost as significantly, though less brutally, in our second age as men have done to women in our third. They kept most men ignorant that they were even needed in the process of procreation. And it wasn't only invading hordes that rose up against the feminine but men within their cultures, as well, as the age weakened, decomposed and went to extremes.

We carry these things in our hidden, collective memory.

Not that one suppression is justified by another, but we must come to understand and accept these things as part of our past and move beyond them instead of having them unconsciously, continually derailing us.

So we must leap again, to a combined functioning of the fourth and fifth chakras, the heart and the throat, where the masculine and feminine come into balance; inclusion, support and acceptance supplant competition; the win-win mentality replaces the win-lose; a newer and higher sense of oneness evolves from the elemental one of the first chakra age; the shepherding, caretaking, honoring impulses of the second chakra are renewed on a global level; and the will evolves from the I, me me, mine/our little group ego to the Us (as in all of us as balanced, fair and equitably redressed as possible) and Thine (as in divine, sublime, generous, charitable and supportive of all—the all-inclusive God/God's will perspective).

Doing what we can to help all sides flower. What a concept! Imagine it!

Ever since the fifties, there has been an attempt to move in this direction.

It flowered in the sixties and into the seventies and then pulled back, almost viciously, to the seeming opposite.

But more and more of us have come to feel that we need to find a new way of being, a new way forward.

It has been feared and treated as rebellion, disparaged as New Age and hoped and worked for as Ascension.

All along, many of us have been talking of the old paradigm and the new.

But our numbers have been small and we've been fragmented, each working our own little, treasured niche.

The old paradigm has definitely become a juggernaut, rampaging out of control.

It is killing us in its death throes, strangling us in its ever-greedier grabbing frenzy.

We have seen some indications of a breath of fresh air.

The Occupy endeavors, the proliferation of non-profits and NGOs, the women's marches, Bernie Sanders surprising not a few.

But can the benevolent coalesce?

How can we coalesce?

What will it take for us to truly accomplish the Herculean task of changing the direction of the human race?

We have already begun.

It could soon begin snowballing.

Quietly, more and more of us have been working within.

Millions of us doing the hard work of healing and evolving.

This has been laying the foundation for the outer changes that will soon have to take place.

The Leap Manifesto offers new potential for a uniting way forward.

Other advanced, activist efforts have manifested.

Around the world, workers are getting together to form their own just entities.

Groups and individuals are coalescing to form new biomolecular models for removing carbon from the atmosphere. And some forward-looking governments are spearheading the move towards renewable energy.

Things will happen at the grass roots level.

There will be unification, especially among the spiritual and activist.

But the details of how our new way forward will unfold remain to be seen.

There is great potential in our young people and in our country.

In terms of our environment, energy, health care and the treatment of our citizens, America has fallen behind.

Way behind.

But we have fallen behind before.

In the early days, Russia outpaced us in the space race.

Then, a determined president and scientific community caught us up with and surpassed them in a very short time.

Now we have fallen behind most of the developed world in all the most important areas.

But we have it within us to show ourselves and the world that we can pull ourselves up by our bootstraps and save our lives and our planet.

Somehow, we must do it soon.

Our current leaders race to do the opposite.

The worst part of our old order arrogance and dysfunction have risen to the forefront top to make themselves as dramatically obvious as they can to as many in the world as possible. We have a Saturday Night Live Executive Branch, a House of Cards Supreme Court and an All in the Family

Congress.

Will enough of us see them clearly enough and take their lessons to boomerang us forward in time?

Have we crouched in order to leap?

That is the question.

And I say yes.

We have magnified cartoon character leaders to the nth degree.

They tower and convulse over our nation.

We have made it harder and harder to ignore our own folly.

In this way, perhaps, we have served ourselves admirably.

I think it's clear that if the great leap occurs, the internet will play a significant role.

Watch *The Internet's Own Boy*.

See what one impassioned genius can do.

I wouldn't be surprised if a few special agents forced Aaron Swartz into his 'suicide' hanging as I feel more than confident that Salvador Allende's 'suicide' and many prison inmate 'suicides' are murders.

Miraculously stopping a foolish, super-constricting, overwhelmingly supported internet bill from passing?

How dare the punk!

Making scientific papers freely available to everyone?

What a terrifying thought!

How could the elite journals continue getting richer?

In the brief time Swartz illegally did this, it proved its titanic potential. With a small window of access to the necessary information, a high school student named Jack Andraka discovered and brought the scientific community a new, life-saving test for pancreatic cancer.

What might happen if we really got so radically progressive as to allow everyone free access to all scientific research?

It's quite simple.

There would be a worldwide knowledge explosion.

Sure, there would be misfires everywhere.

But miracles would also happen.
Brilliant solutions would flower all over the planet.
A snowballing knowledge free for all…
Perish the thought!
How frightening!
The elite would become less elite!
The controllers couldn't control the money flow!
A levelled playing field!
Blasphemy!
Treason!
A breakdown of the system!
Our entire, corrupt infrastructure would be threatened!
Such things must be stopped dead in their tracks!
We do usually murder the best of us, don't we?
If Swartz really was offed and this somehow reaches a perpetrator, confess.
Let this come out into the open.
All the rot must come forth.
But perhaps he truly did, under the intense pressure he was being assaulted with, take his own life. What a tragedy that the small, vindictive ugliness of our system caused such a thing.
What loss and travesty!
The world is full of uncountable travesties.
But we are not helpless to do anything about them.
We can each do so very much.
Far more than we know.
It really does begin as an inside job.
More of this below.
But in this context, may everyone, everywhere with privileged information about any corruption, confess.
It's the most patriotic, honorable thing you can do.
We can't clean it out when it's so expertly hidden.
Covert operations are a major symptom of our disease.
They despoil us from within.
Why so many shootings and pedestrian run downs so often now?
They're coming almost every day.

Why so many opioid deaths?

Why so many suicides?

Why the anti-depressant pandemic, the mass pain killer addictions?

Why the massive, plugged-in screen addictions?

What a waste, though the latter will help drive the revolution.

There's something rotten in the state of America.

We must expose it all to come clean.

Do it for the sake of your own soul and the health and well-being of our nation.

Come forward.

Be a true hero.

So much evil we have done in the name of freedom and to feed our greed.

In Chile and so many South and Central American countries, in Cuba, Haiti, Granada and the Dominican Republic, to the Native Americans, the Hawaiians and the Africans in hundreds of years of slavery, in Korea, Iran, Vietnam, Iraq and Afghanistan, travesties that have and will reverberate down through the decades and centuries.

We have swaggered around the world, looting and stealing everything we could.

Who could withstand us?

We have had our way with nearly everyone.

We have projected the evil empire onto others.

But it is we who have been and continue to be the evil empire, the preeminent raper of the world.

Read Smedley Butler's famous *War Is a Racket* quote.

Oh hell, let's quote him here from his 1935 book via WikiQuote.

Like all the members of the military profession, I never had a thought of my own until I left the service. My mental faculties remained in suspended animation while I obeyed the orders of higher-ups. This is typical with everyone in the military service.

War is a racket. It always has been. It is possibly the oldest, easily the most profitable, surely the most vicious. It is the only one international in scope. It is the only one in which the profits are reckoned in dollars and the losses in lives.

There are 40,000,000 men under arms in the world today, and our statesmen and diplomats have the temerity to say that war is not in the making. Hell's bells! Are these 40,000,000 men being trained to be dancers?

A few profit – and the many pay. But there is a way to stop it. You can't end it by disarmament conferences. You can't eliminate it by peace parleys at Geneva. Well-meaning but impractical groups can't wipe it out by resolutions. It can be smashed effectively only by taking the profit out of war.

I spent 33 years and four months in active military service and during that period I spent most of my time as a high class muscle man for Big Business, for Wall Street and the bankers. In short, I was a racketeer, a gangster for capitalism. I helped make Mexico and especially Tampico safe for American oil interests in 1914. I helped make Haiti and Cuba a decent place for the National City Bank boys to collect revenues in. I helped in the raping of half a dozen Central American republics for the benefit of Wall Street. I helped purify Nicaragua for the International Banking House of Brown Brothers in 1902-1912. I brought light to the Dominican Republic for the American sugar interests in 1916. I helped make Honduras right for the American fruit companies in 1903. In China in 1927 I helped see to it that Standard Oil went on its way unmolested. Looking back on it, I might have given Al Capone a few hints. The best he could do was to operate his racket in three districts. I operated on three continents.

This is America.

The best criminals in the world.

This is the art of the deal our currently elected leader exemplifies and extols.

Grab everything, screw everyone.

As royally as possible.

And celebrate our moral, ethical bankruptcy.

Kind of goes along with grabbing pussies.

Conquer and rape.

The hallmark of the patriarchal age.

This is what we have mostly done in the world while portraying ourselves as the benevolent saviors.

Butler's words have had little impact.

But it's time to let understanding seep into our souls.

It's time for us to come to grips with all we have done and are doing, to take it to heart and own up to it all and, especially, to uncover what has, till now, been kept hidden.

It's time to realize that this paradigm no longer serves us.

But here's the thing.

Despising Trump, the patriarchy or this whole mind set and everyone in it also doesn't serve us.

Look how far the patriarchal age has gotten us.

It's yielded millennia and especially centuries of amazing progress.

And, yes, America has been better at it than most everyone else.

But it's simply a stage of development, an evolutionary rung on the ladder that all of us have gone through in one life or another whether we believe that or not. (Or, if you don't wish to accept this, think of it as a stage of awareness that many of our fellow humans currently occupy and can evolve beyond.)

But we can't become great (again) by going back to it, by resorting to it over and over again in ever more obscene ways.

<u>It No Longer Serves Us</u>!

<u>IT IS NOW DESTROYING US</u>!

Trump's error is that he exemplifies this now dysfunctional way of being and hasn't a clue that there's anything better.

So he wants to make us great again by reinforcing and super-maxing what has worked for him and us in the past.

Not such terrible motivation…

But, now, he's dead wrong.

He's blinded by the old paradigm.

Or, more accurately, he simply hasn't yet evolved to the point where his higher chakras have kicked in allowing a more universal identity field and deeper, more timely understandings to emerge within him.

This is how we grow as individuals, groups and a species. We hold onto archaic mindsets and keep on engaging in counterproductive behaviors long before we wise up enough to finally catch on and kick those habits—and even then, those habitual tendencies keep arising within us, though less and less frequently over time.

In the current overall state of our human evolution, Trump has become primitive man.

He and so many others…

(His recent proclamation that he is a stable genius reverberates to memory Nixon's that he wasn't a crook, does it not?)

Unfortunately, the Republican Party has been almost completely taken over by primitive, self-serving men, many of whom violently adhere to the sad article of faith in an apocalypse that decimates the world and everyone in it but their own few brethren. So nothing should be done to save the planet. Everything that furthers its destruction is in God's will who, it seems, has created in order to destroy it all on behalf of a few personal friends.

In choosing Trump and them to lead us, we took the proverbial step backward, albeit a giant one, in order, hopefully, not to take two steps but to take our necessary great leap forward.

Unfortunately, most Democrats, including Hillary and Obama, were also in the corporate pocket.

So, besides Bernie, who didn't fly out of the starting gate fast enough but who showed that there's more hope than people realized, we didn't have much choice.

What we might see is that there is enough evolutionary force in the Republican Party for it to implode in the next two years and that someone in the Democratic Party like Bernie or better will emerge in time for 2020. (Hmm, Oprah? We've done worse. How about with Elizabeth Warren as VP? Now that would be a leap! Oprah and Pocahontas—she could take the nickname Trump meant to be derogatory as a badge of honor whether or not she does, indeed, have Cherokee blood. Why, after all, would her family make that up and does it matter? Though Winfrey and Warren does have a more dignified, alliterative ring. Though, forgive me, Oprah may or may not have the substance we really need.)

We might even see a wave of recalls removing wrongdoers from office, besides, of course, the ones that have already happened due to #MeToo.

Inspiring, huh?

A modern-day witch hunt but a valid one where the victims are corrupt 'representatives' who despise the will of their constituents and only represent themselves and their ilk.

Or perhaps the government will do something so egregious that we'll have a ten-million-person march, occupy their offices and terrify them into doing the right thing.

But these are either prescience or simple fantasies. We can't wait for, depend on or place too much emphasis politicians. They're gleefully dancing us to destruction. And statesmen are as scarce as hen's teeth. Though if one comes along, by all means, vote her in.

We must rise up as a people and do something. Because, for the first time in history, we have come to the point where our inertia threatens our very existence.

So back to 'great.' There is great and there is great. We won't become great by putting ourselves foremost, denying climate change and bilking everyone else and the world as much as we can.

Nor will we become great (dear Hillary and Naomi) by throwing everyone gripped by that mindset (or waiting to evolve) in 'a basket of deplorables' or by trying to 'kill the inner Trump'—those tendencies within us.

We all have them to a smaller or larger degree.

We grow by accepting and incorporating all the good and the bad we have learned from the past and not letting the bad rule us, by remembering where it led us, by carrying our lessons with us, by embracing a better, more productive functioning, by appreciating the totality of all we and others are without condoning or indulging in the worst of it, without trying to obliterate what we can't help but still carry within us, by simply letting go, as much as we can, what no longer serves us.

We will become greater than ever by taking the leap into a new, higher stage of development and realizing that that is all it is.

That we might have all kinds of tendencies but we choose to live by the best in us.

That those still living less evolved modes are not despicable, just as we are not for still having some of those tendencies.

That, perhaps, somewhere at some time we lived what 'they' are living and 'we' can reach out to 'them' as best we can to help them make the leap, as well, that Trump is not the 'other,' the enemy, he's just misguided and living the stage of development he's living (and is serving us well by being an overblown, comic book version of where we are now going wrong).

That in hating and denigrating 'them,' we have polarized ourselves and helped bring them to power. (We do empower what we fear, dismiss, hate or try to annihilate, whether it's those out there or our own internal impulses.)

Speaking of impulses, I may be drawn to beautiful, erogenous zones and wish to feel them. For better and worse, most of us are wired that way.

Hating them or trying to kill them only exaggerates them.

The question is, do I act on those desires without permission?

Do I honor 'the other' or degrade her?

Do I make her a contemptable object?

That depends on whether I'm gripped by the second, third or fourth chakra, among other things.

In the early stages of third chakra functioning, she is still 'the other,' an object of ownership, hardly human (just as Columbus couldn't grok that our country's indigenous might be equal or even, in some ways, superior to him. It gets quite complicated because there's a great deal of development that occurs in every chakra stage along multiple prongs of our variegated personhood. It usually takes many lifetimes to progress through one chakra before we become ready to move on to the next, though this is a time of great acceleration. And it's further complicated by overlap where we're straddling two chakras or more).

As the fourth and fifth chakras awaken, our identity fields, thankfully, expand to encompass 'them.'

(At this point in the evolution of our species, women, in general, are more highly evolved than men, though, in making the leap we will catch up. Hopefully we'll see more waves like #MeToo and #TimesUp having widespread impact in all sectors of our society as more women galvanize and also take on world leadership roles.)

So, again, despising and trying to kill those impulses within me is counterproductive.

It creates internal war, feeds and pressurizes the impulses and leads to them coming out in direct misbehavior or sideways.

I am far better served by realizing and accepting that I will have them, clarifying the distinction between impulse and action, letting the desire flow through me and subside without driving me to overt, inappropriate action and cultivating the maturity and restraint to disallow the arrogant violation of the other's sovereignty and sacred space, whether it be woman, man, attribute-specific bloc or country.

Rape, in whatever form, hating and killing are not our way forward.

Hating Trump and ethno, gender, faith or race-centric people is counterproductive.

Hating each other is counterproductive.

Party-centric, party line, contra-party animosity is destroying us.

It adds to our collective contempt, which is a very real thing and has gone through the roof.

What's happened to American individualism?

Are we so identified with our political party that we have lost our humanity?

We each are at our own level of development.

Don't we all have all kinds of impulses and tendencies?

Don't we nearly all have profoundly wounded inner children and arrested development?

(And if you don't, God bless you. It might serve you well to sit down and profoundly imagine what it's like from time to time—and to really see if you don't.)

Internally befriending, though not necessarily condoning or acting on, everything within and without but choosing to live by our higher light and, when we can, helping others evolve and grow wiser when they're open to it is what is needed.

Finding, within us, our deeper comprehension and compassion is our only way forward.

Realizing that there is an inner hierarchy of evolution, the activation and empowerment of each successive higher chakra, which leads us to ever more universal embodiment and higher virtues, and that as this happens for each one, the lower ones are incorporated, not nullified.

Awakening to the understanding that despising those at previous stages or those more primitive tendencies within us damages our own selves and holds us back.

Unearthing, embracing and accepting all that we've done wrong and all those who cling to the old ways and moving on from there is what will help us become even greater than we ever have been (in a real, honest way as opposed to a grandiose).

We're all in the same sinking ship.

We need as many of us as possible to start bailing and throwing out the ballast instead of adding to it.

Hate divides. Hate pollutes. Hate undoes us.

And pushing our more highly evolved knowing on others without their exhibiting some kind of receptivity also won't help. (No single quotes because more advanced levels of development really are more highly evolved and it's impossible to refer to them without sounding elitist. We are more highly evolved than the Neanderthal, are we not? Is that elitist? And we Sapiens really do come with built in evolutionary stages of development that we all grow through and it's time we more fully crystalized and appreciated them.

The march of evolution doesn't stop, though its advance through less obviously measurable identity, virtue and energy levels—the evolution of the individual and collective spirit—might be more debatable or difficult for many to appreciate or accept.

Ultimately, we are all equal. Each soul is precious and counts. But it always has been and always will be that some people are prettier, more intelligent, more knowledgeable, physically stronger, more privileged, more decent, more famous or more highly evolved or less so than most others. It's just that we're not as used to thinking of and working on the latter as on all the former. It's at this stage in our evolution as a species that larger and larger numbers of us are meant to become more so. We do need a revolution in consciousness and a sea change in policies if we are to survive.)

So, obviously, I am elitist, as we all, in some way or another, inevitably are. I'm for the really, truly best in us and being the best that we can be—best—defined as being honest, decent, honorable and upright as opposed to being the best at taking advantage of others.

This is key and bears repeating. In wanting to be the best again, we elected as our leader a rip-off artist, one of the best at the art of the win-lose deal, blatantly championing stealing, getting the most and giving the least, screwing over the other, what we, as a nation, have mostly been doing in the world. This is hypocritically 'best,' the best at being immoral, not truly best. This degrades us all, creates imbalance and pollutes our being and our habitat. This makes us thieves and rapers. This creates enemies. And rip-off artists have no compunction about floating any lie that will serve their cause—them, their clique or, in this case, purportedly, their nation. But this doesn't change anything, it just expands the arena. Making us the first in the world at all other nations' expense can't work anymore.

The world has evolved too far along for that. It will only destroy us. We have to learn to work together.

In the larger picture, lying, stealing, blustering and denying won't make us great.

Only acknowledging the truth of our situation and doing everything we can to correct it will.

Regarding deal-making, we become more truly best by making it win-win, finding the highest solution that benefits all parties, championing the honorable vs. the rip-off deal.

In the win-lose deal the antagonist despises the 'other,' makes him his inferior, opponent or enemy and does his best to best him, take all one can from him, vanquish him. Again, he functions from the third chakra—competition, separation, superiority, conquest, hate.

In the win-win deal, one values the other, approaches him or her as a potential partner and finds the best way to bring about mutual benefit, whether it's in business or relationship. It elevates integrity and respect to a higher level than power, sex or money, where they belong. It nourishes the soul as well as the pocketbook. It honors all parties, trashes no one and enriches the world. Though the bottom line profit or sexual gratification might be less, this is being our truly best. Higher chakra functioning—collaboration, unity, equality, balance, love—has superseded lower. The negotiator has evolved but can still discern the level of evolution of the other and act accordingly so as not be taken advantage of herself.

It's been said that America went from barbarism to decadence without knowing civilization. It's time for us to become civilized, a true statesman in the world as opposed to a corrupt politician, dominator or thief. This is how we can renew ourselves and lead the way.

So we have to be truly wiser, more humble, more honest, more humorous, more compassionate, more understanding, more tolerant and more loving, forgiving and tactful all at the same time.

(Also, being simply civil, respectful and polite will help.)

In a word, saint-like.

Without sacrificing our true personhood, strength and authenticity.

Sound impossible?

It's not.

The good news is that's where we're all headed whether we do what we can to evolve or do everything we can not to.

And all any of us can do is the best we can.

So going back to dear Aaron Swartz and all our corruption and covert operations, if you have anything that hasn't yet come to light, do your patriotic duty.

Trumpet the whistle.

Take it to the press.

Give it to WikiLeaks.

Put up a video on YouTube.

Do it with as much publicity as possible.

Save our souls.

Help us evolve.

Even if it means the end of your career.

Even if it means martyrdom or imprisonment.

Death is not the end.

There are more important things than clinging to safety, greed and misplaced loyalty.

There are even more important things than clinging to our current bodies.

What would it do to our national psyche if the CIA, FBI, NSA, Homeland Security, Pentagon and whoever made public every operation they have ever performed or planned—like that one from the sixties to perpetrate an act of terror on national soil and blame it on Cuba so we could invade them? Where would our own operatives have hit, South Beach? I'd sure like to know.

You do know that the Gulf of Tonkin incident, our excuse for invading Vietnam that led to the resolution sanctioning us to do so, was totally fabricated, do you not—that our criminal invasion of that sovereign nation was based on a lie just as our criminal invasion of Iraq was based on the lie of their having and being about to use weapons of mass destruction? No wonder Johnson decided not to run again. Perhaps he did have a conscience after all.

Covert operations and not knowing leads to insanity on both sides. I wouldn't be surprised if Johnson somehow knew of and colluded in Kennedy's assassination—it was his state. Just as I wouldn't be surprised if Bush and Cheney knew about and colluded in 9/11—if so, what sweet, innocent cover they staged for Bush, to have him sitting in a children's classroom while Cheney was in some command post bunker when it happened.

And isn't it true that the Corps of Army Engineers knew that New Orleans was in danger but that they and the highest ups did nothing so the next storm could wipe out as many Big Easy 'deplorables' as possible? They even got police on bridges to shoot those fleeing for their lives.

And then there's the CIA cold-bloodedly flooding our American ghettoes with crack cocaine supplied by their Nicaraguan rebel army buddies and probably the Medellin Cartel so they could kill two birds with one stone—murder, weaken and mass incarcerate millions of blacks in coordination with Reagan's new War on Drugs so as to permanently control and marginalize as many people of color as possible as they blocked local efforts to investigate where the drugs were coming from and raise funds for their covert war in Nicaragua. Brilliant, no? What fun they must have had with this one. How proud they must have been! It worked so well—the War on Drugs which was really the War on Blacks.

We've known about the coke for decades. The CIA admitted it in 1998. Though, of course, no one was charged or prosecuted even though they were breaking the laws the War on Drugs was supposed to enforce. For them to run massive amounts of cheap, illegal, quick-fix drugs was 'legal'. One tiny example of the legalized crime our system has become.

But the massive criminality and lowbrow, malevolent cunning behind our beloved Gipper's bland, personable mask has, for most of us, only now really come to light. Reagan instituted ways to send massive amounts of federal funds and astronomical numbers of heavy duty military armaments to state and local police forces throughout the country as incentive packages to spur them on to make as many drug arrests as possible and further incentivized them by allowing them to simply confiscate, without due process, and keep for themselves cash, cars, drugs, paraphernalia, houses and even Lear Jets if they might have had anything to do in any way with even the most minor drug infractions. Legalized police theft. Think that might ever be abused? (Watch *Molly's Game*.)

This is what exploded the number of police force SWAT teams in our country and their excessive use of wanton military violence to terrorize children, grandmothers and, of course, young, black men.

What an example of the deeply embedded, behind the scenes Molotov cocktails that our beloved leaders can come up with in conjunction with the power they can wield with covert criminals at their disposal. Reagan basically induced our police forces to become violent thieves by legalizing forced, criminal entry and confiscation, though many did not succumb to the call.

And he named Russia the Evil Empire! This, dear friends, is abuse of power and projection magnified to the presidential degree. These kinds of things can't be allowed to go on unrecognized, unchecked and unpunished.

Meanwhile, Nancy is mouthing her platitude 'Just Say No' and, in contradistinction, on the side of intelligent, enlightened, efficacious decency, Portugal decriminalizes all drugs and uses their funding for prevention and treatment. Ten years later they are able to report a dramatic decrease in drug use, HIV infection and drug-related crime.

Duh…

ISN'T IT OBVIOUS?

WHY ISN'T IT OBVIOUS?

Because third chakra programming is mostly limited to hating, murdering, expunging, suppressing, punishing and controlling.

Michelle Alexander, God bless her, (maybe she could be Oprah's running mate or run for the office, herself) came out with a new, thorough elucidation of this in her recent book, *The New Jim Crow*. Many prison authorities are trying to keep it out of the hands of the inmates who have been so used. For, of course, they have no rights and, God forbid, they should have access to the truth of their condition.

And how many more?

What's happening with all that opium in Afghanistan? Is that part of the reason we're there and have chosen to remain there for so very long, to make money and subdue Americans by feeding their opiate addiction?

For the sad truth is this. Many of those in the highest levels of power who talk of wanting to end drug use, really want to use it to weaken the people most likely to rise up against them. They purposely want to kill, addle and marginalize large segments of the populace so as to feel safer and surer of their control. They want to do everything they can to ensure they keep winning and the people keep losing.

Remember the use of the drug Soma in Aldous Huxley's *Brave New World*? That's what we have here. Keep them weak, stupid, helpless, in line, in jail and rightless. God knows what they'd do if we helped them!

But let's say none of these things are true. Let's go into deep denial as so many do. It is shocking and hard to accept, isn't it? We're the 'good guys,' right?

Just knowing what we've created and that covert operations exist makes this kind of 'mental disease' inevitable. It all truly does corrode national trust.

Did you know that national trust is a crucial element of national health?

It is hard to think of these things in terms of a nation.

But the real truths we know at the depths of our being apply to and impact nations and the world just as readily as they do individuals.

What precious little national trust we have left. What precious little we deserve. What sick puppies we really are. So again, shame on us. Let's learn. Let's do something about it. Let's evolve.

We can't change the past, but we must face, acknowledge, apologize and make amends for what we have done so we can move on and do better.

We must own up.

We must wake up.

We must grow up.

Initially, total disclosure would be shocking and devastating. But soon it would wake us up and purge us to our greatest benefit. So while we're at it, let's demand it and an end to all these corrupt secret practices.

It is not in our highest national good to have groups of black op drug runners and assassins above the law who can, in utter secrecy, perpetrate any crime because in someone's mind it is in our national interest, even and especially if that someone happens to be the president.

And this, too, how many despicable things have we done in the name of our 'national interest' that have made that phrase the darkest of euphemisms? Just because we've been doing these things doesn't mean we must continue. We must replace them and the corrupt mentality behind them with something better. We must become something better. Only then can we lead the way to renewal, sanity and well-being as opposed to the oblivion we race to.

We can still spy on enemies but only act through overt channels when allowed by due process or, in true emergencies, only acting with subsequent total disclosure.

Remember due process?

Remember habeas corpus?

Holding anyone for decades or even years without trial is another one of our current practices devouring the health of our national soul.

And then there's torture—do the good guys torture people or knowingly send them to it?

I'm one of those rare people who believes that kindness will turn 'enemies' and criminals more effectively than degradation and torture, though they still must be stopped from harming others.

Treat them well.

Be a role model.

Blow their minds.

Give them this book to read.

Flood the prisons with *The New Jim Crow*.

It's time for us to stop being so despicable.

Drug use should not be a reason to be in jail.

The wealthy, elite, privileged get their fixes legally from the pharmaceuticals through doctors. Or they use the illegal ones with impunity.

The poor are the most vulnerable and easily punishable.

This must end.

Prisons breed crime and the move among the experts before the War on Drugs, when so many fewer were in them, was to reduce their number, not exponentially increase it. In prisons for profit, we have reached a new low. They were part of the whole War on Drugs blueprint.

Only the proven dangerous should be in humane, public prisons—those who have perpetrated violence against others, including rape, who use weapons to steal or who design plots that could cause destruction.

The War on Drugs was a crime from the get go.

All drugs should be carefully and intelligently regulated and made legal.

Prostitution should be made legal.

We can't legislate this kind of 'immorality' out of existence.

Haven't we learned that yet?

We learned it of alcohol through prohibition.

Now we must learn it for the rest.

All those who have been arrested for nonviolent, drug related crimes should be freed, exonerated and given all their rights back as should all felons who have paid their debt to society.

The New Jim Crow undercaste should be abolished.

It's society's crimes and failings that have caused their plight.

Its victims need help, not marginalization and more punishment.

There should be restitution for setting them up in the first place and they should be taught the tools of redemption and helped into the mainstream economy, not barred from it.

And any attempt to block any citizen from voting should be categorized as a felonious act of violence. And those who attempt to do so should have their rights taken away until they have paid their debt to society. Every person's right to vote should be made sacrosanct.

And while we're at it, let's abolish the Electoral College. Our dear Republic has never really worked all that well. It's always been there to protect the rich. The rich have always fleeced and disempowered the poor but we don't have to fleece them. We just have to set things up in a fair, just and balanced way so that the power and wealth they have amassed is tempered with some of it wisely redistributed to the benefit of all.

It's time for a true Democracy with our President being elected by real popular vote—every citizen who wants one getting an equally counting vote no matter where they may live.

(One vote per email address with those without invited to get one at their local library? Could such a thing be monitored and kept from being feloniously manipulated? And then we could vote on everything important this way. Mark Landau's happy, healthy, just, enlightened, highly-evolved, mostly drug-free Brave New World...:)

I'll eventually get to how we could begin to bring this about now.

Please do keep reading.

4 EXPONENTIALISM

Or exponential expansionism.

When the human race gets to the end of an age it goes somewhat berserk and pushes the long-held tendencies of that age to the limit.

This is what is now happening with our patriarchal, third chakra functioning.

At one extreme, the greed, power-in-the-world, self-aggrandizing maneuvers of the most successful few are expanding exponentially.

Extreme third chakra functioning.

At the other end of the spectrum, the incompetent, frustrated, rage-filled, despairing, helplessly-thwarted few are killing themselves or everyone they can.

Extreme third chakra functioning.

All along the middle, the rest of us mostly anaesthetize ourselves in all the manners of our choosing and shake our heads over what might possibly be done.

Not so extreme but still dysfunctional third chakra functioning.

Just a little snapshot of our current state of exponentialism.

But let's be a bit fairer to ourselves.

It had to come to this.

To jump from one age—one phase of evolution—to another is no mean feat.

It takes great compression and rupture.

So let's celebrate.

This is where we are.

Let's rupture into a whole new way of functioning.

Our time demands it.

The potential for the great leap is enormous.

And if we make it, wonderful things will result, miraculous, too-good-to-be-true, though there will be a lot of detritus, as well.

One thing that must happen to counterbalance this giant over-bloat and counter-reaction is for exponentialism to move from the outer realms of the world—money, aggression and worldly power—to the inner realms of our being.

Another thing that must happen is that we must move from too-big-to-fail entities that only shuffle money, make insurance and investment bets, add nothing of real value to our world and super-reward the tip of the pyramid to smaller, democratically owned, producing entities that provide things of true value to the world and allow all its members to thrive.

But let's look at the former for a moment.

We are hitting the ceiling of worldly dysfunction.

What does this mean?

Where do we go from here?

If we go on as we have, it'll be downhill.

Let's stop and take a breath.

Literally.

Stop.

Take a breath.

Take a deep breath.

Take an even deeper breath.

Slow waaaaaay down.

What are you?

Really.

What is a human being?

We think we know.

But do we?

To thine own self be true.

What self?

Know thyself.

Yes, surely, but how?

Ramana Maharshi recommended asking oneself the question, 'Who am I?' in a deeply profound mode of contemplation and exploration.

He also allowed himself to go through a profound death experience at the age of seventeen.

You might try these things but, generally, they don't often work that well for others.

But let's do a little of this right now.

Because somehow, one way or another, our sense of self must exponentially expand.

It can, you know.

We are gripped with this idea that you only live once and then it's over.

Rather bleak, don't you think?

And, if so, why care for anything but our own gratification?

What, then, does integrity matter?

Or then we go to heaven or hell.

So, again, why give a shit about the world?

What could it matter to us then?

Sure, our kids, but then they'll die and it'll be over or they'll go to heaven or hell.

So we're back where we started.

Aren't we more than this?

Really, aren't we?

Yes, we are.

Yes, you are.

You are eternal.

You are multi-dimensional.

You are more than you dream of in your philosophy.

You exist in ways and places you can't begin to fathom.

Though, actually, you can begin to fathom.

You must begin to fathom.

Your sense of self can expand to encompass everything, the entire world and everyone and everything in it, the entire universe, all the universes, all time, space and evolution.

You are a vast, infinite, eternal being.

You are a microcosm and the macrocosm.

And you've had intimations of this.

They can be scary.

We shy away from them.

It frightens us.

We abhor the void.

We abhor the vast infinite.

We abhor the eternal.

But the time has come to embrace it all.

We can.

We must.

I write of these things in *End the Fight*.

I offer a way forward in *What We Can Do*.

We all must heal and evolve in deeper ways than we're used to.

Let's join hands and take the leap together.

One way or another, we will.
We're already being pulled along.
We're already in free fall.
Headlong into the downward spiral.
Or into the upward.
Shall we go down flailing?
Or rise up like the phoenix?
Which would you prefer?

Sooner or later, one way or the other, we'll either be forced to choose or the choice will be made for us.

As things stand, the choice is already being made for us.

5 VALUISM

Black lives matter.
    Red lives matter.
    Yellow lives matter.
    Gypsy lives matter.
    Jewish lives matter.
    Arab lives matter.
    Rwandan and Rohingyan lives matter.
    All lives matter.
    Human beings are more important than corporations.
    More important than money.
    More important than ideologies.
    We are not just cogs in the wheel.
    Dispensable.
    Robotic drones.
    Corporate things.
    Cannon fodder.
    Life is only cheap when we make it so.
    And even then, it's not.
    We pay dearly in terms of the quality and well-being of our souls and mundane existence when we trample the sanctity of life.
    So you matter.
    And you can do more for all of us than you know.

There are things you can do that would help us all.
The more you do them, the more we move towards the leap.
Take better care of yourself.
Eat better.
Breathe better.
Medicate less.
Veg out less.
Drop bad habits.
Incorporate good ones.
Meet and be with your fear and pain.
Meditate.
Three times a day.
Every day.
Forgive yourself, everyone and everything.
Connect with your heart.
Learn better how to love.
Do something in the world to benefit others.
Each one of us who does any or all of these things helps us all.
We have lost the flow.
We have lost the divine vibration.
It is there.
These things help us grow more attuned to it.
We have drowned it out with our consumerism and misery.
With our jadedness.
With our cynicism.
With drugs, alcohol and entertainment.
But it can't be expunged.
It is divine.
It is eternal.
It can sing our lives to a better place.
Whatever religion you may or may not be, life is sacred.
We have stopped treating it as such.
We desecrate it.
We monetize it.

We monetize everything.

The world is not a soulless machine, it is a living being.

You are not a soulless machine.

At the end of the third chakra age, we have overdone the work ethic.

We are not drones.

We have overdone our war machine and the military.

When we make so many brainless killing machines, is it surprising that the tormented resort to murder?

We have abandoned truth.

We have abandoned honesty.

Our chosen leader will say any ridiculous thing.

We have, to an alarming degree, abandoned our very humanity.

We have lost our sense of what is truly of value.

We are in cognitive, moral free fall.

The cow of dharma stands on her head.

When our Environmental Protection Agency becomes our Worst Pollution Licensing Agency and our Supreme Court bars workers from launching class-action lawsuits against employers and rules in favor of restricting our right to vote, we have messed up our values beyond the surreal.

But at the depths of our being they remain inviolate.

We must rejuvenate, bring them to the fore and act on them.

The profane has trumped the sacred.

But we can turn this around.

We can move from Devaluism to Valuism, from de-sanctifying everything to re-sanctifying everything.

We can reinvigorate production with love, decency and development.

We must relearn how to truly care for ourselves, for each other and for our planet.

Life is precious.

It is threatened.

Nothing less will do.

6 MILITARISM

Nothing epitomizes third chakra function like Militarism.

Destroy, maim and kill for the greater good.

Martin Luther King was our most beautiful spokesman for the new paradigm.

So, of course, he was murdered.

He said many true, profound things, but let's look at this one:

"A nation that continues year after year to spend more money on military defense than on programs of social uplift is approaching spiritual doom."

We continue to do this every year so, more and more, we live spiritual doom, a sense of helplessness, mass malaise.

And we do precious little defense.

But oh how we love offense!

And mostly to enhance our own abilities to do business where and how we please.

As Michael Moore's film title so aptly put it, *Where To Invade Next?*

We spend more on invading other countries, on military offense, than on anything.

We spend more than the next seven nations combined.

We are the great perpetrator.

How sick can we get?

Sicker, believe me.

It's true that al-Qaeda and ISIS are violent, repressive and hopelessly backward, but, to a large degree, we created them.

By imposing the Shah on Iran, building bases in Saudi Arabia, invading Iraq and Afghanistan and being so rabidly pro-Israel, we ensured the buildup of violent reaction.

If we were invaded and occupied by a foreign power who imposed their way of life and business on us, would we sit quietly?

Most of us probably would but wouldn't some insurgents rise up in violence to attack the foreign devils?

Hello…

Are we awake?

Have our brains been washed or have they been bleached and dry cleaned?

Are we seeing through a glass darkly or are we stone cold blind?

Will we allow the scales to fall from our eyes?

Or have we simply become hopeless, brainless, non-caring beasts?

What gives us the right to invade and impose our will on them?

Our might?

Because we are divinely right?

Manifest destiny?

Because we deserve what few resources and little money they have?

Are we bringing democracy to the world?

Was the Shah democracy?

Were the corrupt, dictator business partners we imposed on uncounted sovereign nations democracy?

When true democracy brought Chile Allende, we assassinated him and replaced him with a monster—covertly, of course.

Or we helped orchestrate his fall before he had a chance to really do what the majority of the people of Chile wanted.

That's how much we love democracy.

We truly are The Ugly American.
And so very proud of it!
And now North Korea.
Korea before and Korea again.
It began with Trump posturing, being belligerent and thus further making them our enemy.
We just have to have an enemy.
It's like we need it to feel big and strong and powerful.
And we love being afraid.
Then he wanted to wade in there and, in his customary fashion, show the world he could overcome his adversary.
But then came the Olympics and in the accelerated evolutionary energy of our current moment, the wily Kim Jong-un slipped out of his grasp and went, apparently and hopefully, straight to the south for unification, a not so small sign and example of the miracles we might see in our rapidly deteriorating old world order.
The Republicans saw this as a great triumph for Trump and, God bless him, he has played part of this somewhat well. But the Nobel prize?
That, if to anyone, should go to Kim.
He is the one who pivoted if, indeed, he follows through.
And now, as of this final edit, they have met and nothing conclusive seems to have changed.
We still have two wacko, unstable, nuclear-capable world leaders whose fingers could push the buttons.
Not a happy situation.
But the potential for peace and unification is still there.
And who are we to dictate who should have the bomb and who should not?
I am for the total obliteration of all nuclear weapons. But, perhaps, there is a kind of coming of age that occurs when a nation develops it, a necessary sobering that goes along with it.
The current nuclear club, of course, doesn't want anyone else to have it. God forbid!
But let's, at least, take a look at everything. We so very wrongly have been taking so very much for granted for so very

long.

However Korea pans out, it's time we faced ourselves and the truth.

We, the colonial victors and powers, split Germany, Vietnam and Korea in two.

And they have shown us the limits of our stupidity and hubris.

Let us look soberly with wide open eyes at all we have done in the world.

And look how outraged we become when some Russians resort to a little social media propaganda during our election.

How dare they!

What hypocrites we are!

We're out of alignment with everything right as we keep telling ourselves how right we are.

We've been living chronic, prolonged cognitive dissonance and it's tearing us apart.

But really, we've been living the third chakra imperative— we must dominate, control, abuse and subdue.

It has served us well, but no longer.

We must mature beyond it if we are to live decently and survive.

If we stopped our naked, violent, cavalier careering in the Middle East and around the world and let each nation follow its own destiny, over time, anti-American hatred and violent reactions against us and what we have put into place would melt away.

If we stopped all covert and overt foreign intervention and focused on developing ourselves, what an invigorated, healthy, vibrant, abundant nation we could become.

We could lead by example instead of subduing by force.

We could finally forswear colonialism.

What would occur if most of the wealth and effort expended on militarism were put to the use of truly making our world a better place?

Miracles.

While strongman politics will continue to trample

democracy in the near term, as we move beyond patriarchal, third chakra functioning, brutal strongmen, strongman groups and strong-arm nations will subside. There will be less and less tolerance for them and they will implode under their own weight.

We can inspire the world toward a better way.

Eisenhower, who put a lot of our war machine in place, ended his presidency by saying, "We must guard against the acquisition of unwarranted influence, whether sought or unsought, by the military-industrial complex."

Needless to say, we have done the opposite.

We have fed it to the max.

We have institutionalized perpetual war.

War is hell.

War is barbaric.

War is a racket.

War is man's greatest stupidity.

We must evolve beyond war.

With so many nuclear weapons poised in readiness, sooner or later one will be used, which, of course, could trigger the use of more.

The current potential of too many being used for the survival of life on earth is too great to continue maintaining.

Too much of our wealth and focus have been stolen to feed the war machine, to enrich the owners of its factories.

We must turn this around.

We must dismantle much of our militarism.

We must remove our bases from Guam, Cuba and wherever they are abhorred by the people on whose soil we have placed them.

Our War on Terrorism isn't the cure. It's license to extend our military wherever we wish.

It's not our job to go into every country on Earth where a leader friendly to the West wants help in subduing opposition.

US soldiers patrolling foreign soil do not generate love and respect for our country.

Four US soldiers were recently killed in Niger.

Why are US taxpayers giving our money for this?

In general, when local pressures arise around the world, the best policy now for foreign imperialists is laissez-faire, do nothing and let the pressures work themselves out as they will.

In cases like the Rohingyan crisis, as many of the wealthy, benevolent, enlightened nations of the world as possible should simply go to the refugee camps and offer to take the percentage of the refugees they feel they can.

This would be the decent, humane, Christian thing to do, wouldn't it? Though the ethno-centric among us would be horrified by this.

In any case, we must reclaim most of the wealth and energy we expend on war and use it for better purposes.

It has brought us spiritual doom and adds to the threat of our physical doom.

If we are able to make the great leap, eventually, the horrors of war will be looked back upon with wonder as the brutal, primitive insanity they are.

Let's imagine a world without war and then do what we must to bring it about.

Perhaps a United Nations so healthy and strengthened that the knowledge of censure or retaliation from the world community's one enlightened, international peace keeping force would deter every nation from invading every other—with all the world's nuclear weapons obliterated.

Or, in the interim, we could transform ourselves from being the perpetrators to being the truly good cops and only using our might to stop the worst predators when the international community agrees it is called for.

Why not?

We have it within us to structure all kinds of better things.

A new age could work wonders.

Eventually, if we evolve enough and reclaim our true, divine nature, we will turn all our weapons into plowshares.

7 ECOISM

For centuries, we have been destroying our soil, polluting our oceans and pumping carbon dioxide into our atmosphere.

We now have the technology to turn this around, dramatically and super-beneficially.

We can restore and supercharge our soil.

We can improve our agricultural productivity by five times or more.

We can skyrocket carbon sequestration by removing CO^2 from the atmosphere and replacing it in the soil where it belongs.

This can and must be part of The Leap Manifesto.

There is a not very eloquent but brilliant molecular biologist conducting research at the Institute for Energy and Environment at the New Mexico State University College of Engineering.

Dr. David C. Johnson has developed a new, super-effective way of increasing farm, desert and rangeland productivity through the development of beneficial soil microbial communities, notably skewing them away from the bacterial and toward the fungal. He calls it Biologically Enhanced Agricultural Management (BEAM) and it dramatically increases carbon sequestration while minimizing carbon respiration and having all kinds of other wonderful, life-supporting benefits.

Innumerable, friendly microbes support our plant, animal and human lives. They not only help us digest our food and assimilate nutrients, but mediate our immune systems, cravings, emotions and most aspects of our biological functioning.

Johnson has discovered an optimal way in which they can supercharge our soil and agricultural life.

In order to create them, he and his wife developed a No-Turn Compost Bioreactor.

It dramatically reduces the amount of water needed, composting time and salinity and produces high quality, nutrient rich, fungal dominated soil and plant super-food with which he has had miraculous results without fertilizer, herbicides and pesticides.

This is from a March 9, 2016, talk he gave at a conference sponsored by Regeneration International called Is Healthy Soil the Solution to Global Warming? To see it, search YouTube for 'Managing Soils for Carbon Sequestration'.

By stripping carbon and the life forces and supports from our agricultural soils, we have reduced the ability of these soils to function optimally. Restoration of soil microbiome population and its structure along with soil carbon promotes the restoration of biological functionality of our soils. By promoting this restoration, we can begin reducing atmospheric CO^2 concentrations. We can begin now at any level in all ecosystems. We can reverse soil loss by restoring and rebuilding our soils. We can slow desertification. We can reduce soil salinization. We can reduce the downstream pollution from the application of agrochemicals. We can restore beneficial insects and pollinating populations. And we can begin restoring our coral reefs and our oceans also. We have a viable technology to reduce greenhouse gases but we cannot accomplish this without a policy that supports its implementation or without the presence of a stable and predictable market. Farmers and ranchers will need to be compensated for their efforts because the transition period is not easy and they can't afford to go out of business trying to do this, so that there's a subsidy at the beginning, but eventually these systems become self-promoting… (and *provide) the best system of emissions reduction to remove or reduce atmospheric CO².*

Most of our current crop of corrupt politicians would neither be able to comprehend nor be willing to implement this. They don't care about what their constituents want. They don't care about what's good for them. They want to weaken and undermine them. They are there to push through what the corporate lawyers want. They are there to take from others all the wealth and power they can.

It's time for us to rise up and force them to do what we want or force them out.

It's time for us to rethink our existence, from the bottom up.

We waste our waste.

Our waste can be put to precious use.

We are so afraid of it that it's difficult for us to comprehend this.

Our human byproducts and dirty water can be reclaimed, made safe and used in BEAM projects.

We can start turning our rangelands and deserts into super-productive gardens of Eden using our own poo and pee.

We can create private, fecund cornucopias using all the runoff from our homes.

We can produce more food than the world needs.

We can produce healthier, more nutritious, delicious food than we have grown used to and reinvigorate our dying bee and beneficial insect populations.

We can turn the world around from carbon out to carbon in.

There are solutions to our dilemmas.

Small groups have already begun to create these oases.

Here in New Mexico, a few Navajo and Water Management Associates came together to turn a gas station seeping raw sewage and sporting filthy portapotties into an ecological wonder where human waste and runoff is made into safe, super-productive agri-food with all the best microorganisms and nutrients to grow native foods and medicinal plants in an adjacent, sandy lot in an optimum, carbon negative way. Four or five more projects are under way.

In other areas, Native Americans are creating their own renewable energy enterprises.

Others around the world are doing similar things.

Can an intelligent coalition of politicians and voters begin to reclaim sane, beneficial policy-making?

Can we reeducate ourselves and free ourselves from our cult of greed, fear and stupidity?

Can we resurrect our agricultural land and start using innumerable plots that have heretofore been underproductive or never used?

Absolutely.

There are enough good-hearted, sensible people in this country to rally around true solutions if enough of us become aware of them.

That's what The Leap is attempting.

Go join at theleap.org.

It's Canadian but it's spreading worldwide.

There is hope for us.

Let's rise to the occasion.

Let's avert the catastrophe that is nearly upon us.

This could be a very exciting time.

We can do it.

8 DEFOSSILISM

Fossil fuel has driven the industrial age.

It drives our cars.

It has made many obscene super-magnates.

It is nonrenewable, pollutes our world and is killing us.

Continuing to plow money and resources into fossil fuel infrastructure is an investment in death.

It's the epitome of the old order.

It's time to defossilize.

We currently have the technology to begin phasing it out.

New technologies will develop.

Racing to do further damage to deplete what remains is not the direction to go.

In many respects, the US has become the most backward developed country.

Scandinavia, The Netherlands, Germany and China are leading the way.

But we can change this.

We have the potential to catch up and surpass them all.

Like BEAM, there are things happening that very few people are aware of.

We still have our Yankee ingenuity, population and landmass.

There has been a concerted effort to depredate our educational system.

The powerful elite abhor a well-educated citizenry.

It has been quite successful.

Large numbers of us champion ignorance, hate science and adore our oppressors.

When significant potential for change begins to bubble to the surface, there will always be those who cling to the old order, who react against it, who dig in and deny.

We have chosen them to rule us.

On November 13, 2017, scientists of the American Institute of Biological Sciences with over 15,000 additional scientist signatories from 184 countries came out with "A Second Notice," a warning letter to humanity stating the necessity of making major changes "to prevent widespread misery and catastrophic biodiversity loss." It came twenty-five years after a warning from the Union of Concerned Scientists with 1700 additional independent signatories in 1992, including most of the then living science Nobel laureates.

It contains charts showing that since 1992, alone, freshwater resources per capita have gone down by over 26%, vertebrate species abundance by nearly 29%, CO_2 emissions have gone up by over 62%, the rate of temperature change by over 167%, human population by over 35%, ruminant livestock population by over 20% and ocean dead zones by over 75%.

To me, ocean death is often brushed over but is one of the most dangerous possibilities we face. Not only do oil spills, mountains of plastic, massive runoff pollution, more sunscreen every day, over fishing and harvesting and the murderous assault of sonic experimentation endanger the balance of life, but the oceans are warming on an elevated curve as the planet does. Much of the world's photosynthesis occurs in our oceans. They supply about half of our oxygen, let alone their cornucopia of seafood. If they (and the bees) go, and we're getting perilously close, all of life on earth will be severely threatened.

The one good news chart shows that ozone depletors have gone down over 68%, the ozone hole being the smallest it's been since 1968.

They go on to say:

...we have unleashed a mass extinction event, the sixth in roughly 540 million years, wherein many current life forms could be annihilated or at least committed to extinction by the end of this century.

...We are jeopardizing our future by not reining in our intense but geographically and demographically uneven material consumption and by not

perceiving continued rapid population growth as a primary driver behind many ecological and even societal threats (Crist et al. 2017). By failing to adequately limit population growth, reassess the role of an economy rooted in growth, reduce greenhouse gases, incentivize renewable energy, protect habitat, restore ecosystems, curb pollution, halt defaunation, and constrain invasive alien species, humanity is not taking the urgent steps needed to safeguard our imperiled biosphere.

As most political leaders respond to pressure, scientists, media influencers, and lay citizens must insist that their governments take immediate action as a moral imperative to current and future generations of human and other life. With a groundswell of organized grassroots efforts, dogged opposition can be overcome and political leaders compelled to do the right thing. It is also time to re-examine and change our individual behaviors, including limiting our own reproduction (ideally to replacement level at most) and drastically diminishing our per capita consumption of fossil fuels, meat, and other resources.

The rapid global decline in ozone-depleting substances shows that we can make positive change when we act decisively. We have also made advancements in reducing extreme poverty and hunger (www.worldbank.org). Other notable progress (which does not yet show up in the global data sets in figure 1) include the rapid decline in fertility rates in many regions attributable to investments in girls' and women's education (www.un.org/esa/population), the promising decline in the rate of deforestation in some regions, and the rapid growth in the renewable-energy sector. We have learned much since 1992, but the advancement of urgently needed changes in environmental policy, human behavior, and global inequities is still far from sufficient.

Sustainability transitions come about in diverse ways, and all require civil-society pressure and evidence-based advocacy, political leadership, and a solid understanding of policy instruments, markets, and other drivers. Examples of diverse and effective steps humanity can take to transition to sustainability include the following (not in order of importance or urgency): (a) prioritizing the enactment of connected well-funded and well-managed reserves for a significant proportion of the world's terrestrial, marine, freshwater, and aerial habitats; (b) maintaining nature's ecosystem services by halting the conversion of forests, grasslands, and other native habitats; (c) restoring native plant communities at large scales, particularly forest landscapes; (d) rewilding regions with native species, especially apex predators, to restore ecological processes and dynamics; (e) developing and adopting adequate policy instruments to remedy defaunation, the poaching crisis, and the exploitation and trade of threatened species; (f) reducing food waste through education and better infrastructure; (g) promoting dietary shifts towards mostly plant-based foods; (h) further reducing fertility rates by ensuring that women and men have access to education and voluntary family-

planning services, especially where such resources are still lacking; (i) increasing outdoor nature education for children, as well as the overall engagement of society in the appreciation of nature; (j) divesting of monetary investments and purchases to encourage positive environmental change; (k) devising and promoting new green technologies and massively adopting renewable energy sources while phasing out subsidies to energy production through fossil fuels; (l) revising our economy to reduce wealth inequality and ensure that prices, taxation, and incentive systems take into account the real costs which consumption patterns impose on our environment; and (m) estimating a scientifically defensible, sustainable human population size for the long term while rallying nations and leaders to support that vital goal.

To prevent widespread misery and catastrophic biodiversity loss, humanity must practice a more environmentally sustainable alternative to business as usual. This prescription was well articulated by the world's leading scientists 25 years ago, but in most respects, we have not heeded their warning. Soon it will be too late to shift course away from our failing trajectory, and time is running out. We must recognize, in our day-to-day lives and in our governing institutions, that Earth with all its life is our only home.

Gee, intelligent, educated, caring minds think alike.

There is one area in which I am not as concerned as the scientists are and that is regarding population growth.

I think it's clear that we'd be better served by a significantly lower population. But I also believe that with new practices like BEAM, Earth can well sustain us all and more.

If enough of us make the leap there will be balancing mechanisms that will come into play wherein inner congruence with our highest good will bring about spontaneous population reduction or, if not, mass viral or plague epidemics will wipe many of us out if our planet becomes too overburdened.

And then there's extra-terrestrial colonization…:)

But we do need a miracle—something that somehow can galvanize our population out of its lassitude, out of its ignorance, out of the grip of the old paradigm.

We do need truly cogent, world-saving policies.

We do need forward-thinking legislators.

We do need a revolution.

We have it within us.

How will it arise?

We need you and as many as possible to get proactive.

9 GOOD GOVERNANCE

A nation's greatest assets are the minds and characters of her people, the education and intelligence of her children and citizens and the development of their hearts, souls and spirit.

There has been a deliberate effort in America to sabotage our educational system and to dumb as many of us down as money could buy.

Those who have stolen from and control us don't want us able to think.

This is one of the great travesties of the end of the patriarchal age.

It has been carried out in a variety of ways but, especially, through limiting the funding, practices and status of education and educators.

In all the high civilizations that have flourished throughout history, teachers have been rewarded and held in high esteem.

Here and now, we mostly treat them like shit.

They are underpaid, undervalued and there are far too few.

When those who seek to do ill want to promote their efforts, they revile others for what they do and come up with names for their policies which are the opposite of what they truly are.

'No child left behind' was a very sad joke. It implemented policies that left as many children behind as possible.

One of the things that must happen if we are to save and improve our world and make the great leap is to resurrect our free, public schools at every level, pre-K to post-graduate.

Bernie Sanders is a fairly good advocate for the new paradigm.

Many of his ideas are sound and necessary.

The idea that government is bad and should be reduced to almost nothing but the military and leave the market to rule all else is dangerous, foolish and untenable.

And trickle-down economics, as has been said (God bless Noam Chomsky), is really trickle-up economics.

There are many things that good government should do.

All people but the poorest and all businesses and corporations, without loopholes, exceptions or offshore havens, should be sensibly taxed in a brilliantly increasing graduated curve reaching to the top to pay for the things an enlightened, benevolent government should manage.

The richest individuals and corporations should be taxed the most, not the least.

The rules should be calibrated to redistribute wealth back from the most over-bloated to the people.

Those who have stolen the most should pay the greatest burden.

Market regulations are necessary.

The prices pharmaceuticals charge, our whole insurance dominated health care system, the wanton gambling in our financial system, so many areas have spun out of control. And now they're rolling back Dodd-Frank…

Less regulation fosters gambling, theft, corruption, bloat and collapse.

Wealth inequality is a disease that rots us from within.

And it is all made possible by the dumbing of America.

What Henry Ford said about our financial system, "It is well enough that people of the nation do not understand our banking and monetary system, for if they did, I believe there would be a revolution before tomorrow morning," could be extended to most of the rest of our system.

Informed, critical understanding of large numbers of citizens is the last thing the powerful few want.

Here in Santa Fe, a Renaissance genius, astronomer, musician, pilot, programmer, chemist with eidetic memory named David Weininger recently died.

He made his fortune in chemistry and molecular informatics and analysis, providing knowledge, advancement and things of true value to the world.

And this should be made key.

Those who gamble and shuffle insurance bets and financial instruments to get wealthy, providing no real benefit to anyone, should be taxed at a significantly higher rate than those who provide true benefit.

Perhaps the best thing Weininger discovered is a molecule that improves cognition, intelligence and the transfer of data from short term memory to long.

He wanted to test, produce and make this molecule, which he called the Cognition Enhancer, available to the public.

But those in power blocked its approval.

He was threatened and told by several prominent politicians that he wouldn't get approval because "enhanced intelligence is not wanted," just as improved education is not wanted.

This is all part of the travesty of where we have gotten ourselves to.

He built a huge, ten-ton steel model sculpture of the molecule outside Daylight Chemical Information Systems, his company building, for all the world to see.

Perhaps, someday, his brainchild will be tested and produced for the benefit of us all.

These are the kinds of miracles that might come about if we're able to straighten up and fly right.

Our government has become malevolent.

The lords of money have bought it and they are

malevolent.

Enough of us, together, can bring about the change necessary to reestablish benevolent government.

Our postal and library systems benefit us all and should be maintained and improved.

Social Security is life-saving for many and should be strengthened.

Most developed nations have proved that good governance provides far better healthcare to all than the rampaging pharmaceuticals, insurance companies, free market doctors, HMOs and hospitals, with their often astronomically inflated pricing, that we are so enamored of.

There should be ample free education to the highest levels for everyone who wants it and our teachers should be better paid and qualified.

Our current, criminal student loan industry should be outlawed, gutted and defunded.

And, of course, our infrastructures are falling apart.

We need a new New Deal.

The great terror we have of the words social and socialist have been inculcated into us by the wealthy, powerful elite who have had their way with us.

The disempowerment of the labor unions they have so succeeded in doesn't serve us.

Mistreating workers so that the pinnacle can gorge undermines our country.

What we truly need is some kind of benevolent Social Democracy or Democratic Socialism.

Making the raw market profit motive our God will not save us.

It is destroying us.

I am no expert or even, in general, a political animal.

But almost no one is saying what I feel must be said.

So into the vacuum I speak.

Even if I speak only to myself.

Perhaps, someday, a benevolent government will make sure that the basic needs of all its citizens are met.

I do believe we are moving towards a world where robotics will generate most of what we need. So if we manage to save ourselves from traumatizing or destroying Life on Earth, eventually there could be enough wealth to provide all those who need it with a truly comfortable living. We might all have happy, clean, roomy habitats and all our necessities, including transportation, could be abundantly available for free.

What might we do if we didn't have to work for a living?

It could be miraculous.

Even now, if we didn't expend so much on war and over-subsidizing the wealthy, for that is what our system has been set up to do, we could provide everyone who needed it with enough income to live a decent, healthy life.

Such concepts would now horrify and be despised by so very many, but why? At least let us envision them.

Living such lives would free everyone to engage in the most fruitful, creative, enjoyable endeavors imaginable and would manifest a more graceful, heavenly existence here on Earth than we've ever come close to.

Each person would have the optimum chance to bring forth the precious, unique things they do have to offer. Over time, something like this could truly come about.

But first...

10 PACS, LOBBYISTS AND THE CONSTITUTIONAL CONVENTION

Our elections are bought and sold.

Our politicians are bribed, massaged and coerced.

It's gotten to the point where corporate lawyers write our laws in inscrutable legalese and the lobbyists give them to Congressmen, many of whom don't bother to read them and wouldn't understand them if they did. Then they become our laws.

Lobbying should be illegal, like fraud and graft.

Wasn't it once called influence peddling?

The decision as to whether or not a law should be passed should be based on expert research, integrity and intelligence, not pressure and money.

Most of our politicians are in the corporate pocket.

Money has overtaken almost everything.

The amount spent on our elections is obscene.

This is one of the greatest areas in which we need reform.

How can we regulate this?

There must be a sensible, effective way.

Citizens United is clearly not it.

We should structure a state-financed way in which bona fide candidates can reach the public and none of them can spend more than in utilizing it.

Should we base the selection of our leaders on how much money they can raise (or have), on how much they have stolen?

Or, if we do, no person or organization should be allowed to donate more than one thousand dollars to a candidate's campaign, including the candidate.

Shall we continue to make money our God?

That's what we're doing.

Nearly seven billion was spent on the 2016 election.

Much of that money came from five families.

Around two billion of it was dark money from groups that don't disclose their donors.

Another aspect of our existence completely out of control.

That's what happens when regulations are stripped.

We've been removing all the good laws and replacing them with bad ones.

But not all PACs are bad.

Wolf-PAC's goal is "To save democracy in the United States by getting a much needed amendment to the U.S. Constitution that will establish elections which are free of the corrupting influence of money in our political system and fair enough that any citizen can run for office, not just millionaires and their allies."

In order to propose the amendment, they must get resolutions passed in thirty-four states, two thirds of our total.

If two thirds of the members of both Houses of Congress were to vote for it, that would also do. But that would never happen when almost all of them have already been bought.

If thirty-four states pass it, it will go to all the states and thirty-eight would have to ratify for it to be adopted.

So far, five states have passed the resolution—California, Illinois, Vermont, New Jersey and Rhode Island.

Many are working to pass it in other states.

So there is the actual possibility that we can bypass our corrupt legislators, President and Supreme Court and straighten out some of the mess we are in.

But it's an uphill battle. There is great fear around

changing our Constitution. There's a long list of seemingly wonderful activist organizations, including Common Cause, the ACLU and even GreenPeace, who seem to be against it. They and others sow fear that in a Constitutional Convention anything could happen. We might gut the Bill of Rights or throw out the whole Constitution—the myth of the out-of-control, runaway convention.

This is ridiculous.

Even these best organizations have their niche. They are vested in the status quo and don't want to upset it. They want their lobbyists to be able to do their jobs so that they might obtain a few more of their coveted goals. They have the money to play the system as it's evolved. They're afraid of something that really might change it.

Those who stand up to oppose Wolf-PAC's resolution are often paid lobbyists themselves, usually quite attractive, good-hearted and seemingly reasonable.

But they're wrong.

They are inside the box saying, "Oh, don't shake it!"

They are old order activism faced with the new and frightened by it.

They're not ready to acknowledge that the box is broken.

We need out of the box thinking and action.

First of all, we're talking about Amendments to the Constitution, not changing the Constitution, itself.

And we can't do this unless we first get thirty-four states to pass the resolution and then thirty-eight to ratify it. Thirty-eight states will not ratify weakening the Bill of Rights or other excellent parts of our Constitution. The amendment won't even be about that.

Saving our planet has gone beyond keeping the status quo, trying to work within it and winning a few goals or little tweaks here and there to try to make things a little bit better.

We need something Earth-shaking.

We need a Great Leap.

We're either intelligent enough to make the changes necessary to turn this runaway train around and set ourselves on a higher, better course or we're not and we might as well kiss our great-grandchildren and our planet goodbye.

We've been shaking up Mother Earth for over a century and we're now pushing her to the brink. And we've been hammering the integrity of our policies and political and legal institutions for almost as long.

Small steps and half-measures won't do.

We must do the big, shake-up things necessary to force the issue and bring about the changes we need.

Wolf-PAC's method is ideal for this.

If fear keeps us from grabbing the bull by the horns and doing what's necessary to survive, then it's fear that will kill us.

We have our Constitution and it's a great one. But it has brought us to our current pass. It is time to make it better. We need new protections from the ultra-modern disasters that we now face.

A Constitutional Convention is exactly what we need and with more than just Wolf-PAC's one amendment to address our multiple new threats.

There has never been one since the first at the inception of our nation. Currently, there are twenty-seven amendments to the Constitution. Except for Prohibition, they're mostly good and reasonable. But everyone has been so afraid of having a Convention that when one has come close in the past, the two houses of Congress have buckled and passed what the states were demanding.

But now we truly would be best served by having a second one. In so doing, gutting the Constitution would not be on the table, only adding at least one amendment to eviscerate the power of money, corporations and lobbyists to control our nation. The other twenty-seven amendments didn't gut the Bill of Rights or destroy the Constitution and neither will this.

But we really do need more than just one amendment.

For almost everywhere we look there truly is a mess.

Such a mess in so many ways.

But a mess that we can and must clean up.

Amendments to our Constitution could be the most

effective way to do this.

So let's have our convention, invite our best, most enlightened constitutional, scientific and public minds and draft a host of nation-changing amendments.

Wolf-PAC is determined to limit themselves to the one amendment and uses that as a selling point to alleviate the fear of a runaway convention. But, perhaps, a wave of enough of us could help them realize our country and our world need more.

Here are some we might consider besides removing money from politics and personhood status from corporations.

Legalize all drugs and prostitution. Free those in prison for nonviolent violation of the ineffective laws regarding them and expunge their criminal records. Dismantle the New Jim Crow matrix, civil forfeiture and the removal of rights from felons who have paid their debt to society. Abolish prisons for profit. And mandate treatment, prevention and educational programs. Criminalizing the damaged, weak and immoral doesn't help. Waging war on them doesn't help. Only helping them will help.

Ensure that every US Citizen, except while serving time, is allowed to vote.

Strengthen our laws against rape and harassment.

Criminalize all forms of lobbying.

Raise the minimum wage to $15.

Stop Monsanto (now Bayer? how innocuous!) and others from polluting or copyrighting our food supply. Establish subsidies for BEAM technology and cover crops. And ban all huge monocrops and the worst polluting pesticides, herbicides, fertilizers and chemicals.

Criminalize Chem trails and all chemical experimentation within a hundred miles of any human habitation.

Ban ocean sonar, sonic experimentation and ocean damaging sunscreen.

Abolish the Electoral College and institute true democracy.

Transfer all Federal Reserve System Bank assets to a newly established Central Bank of the USA, owned by the people, to print currency and set interest rates. Or remove it from private ownership by nationalizing it.

Too big to fail is too big to continue. Break up the biggest monsters and place sensible caps on what can be paid to all highest ups.

Mandate the separation of commercial and speculative banking.

Mandate net neutrality.

Split the difference between Daylight Savings and Standard Time, go to the half hour and never change the time again so that Eastern Time would always be four-and-a-half hours behind Universal. Changing the time twice a year is just another thing that weakens us. It disrupts our biological clocks and rhythms and sends the message that we're nothing but robotic dogs.

Recall all operatives from foreign soil, disclose all past and present Top-Secret operations and plans and end all covert actions.

Establish a timetable for ending all new fossil fuel infrastructure investment and all fossil fuel use where possible. Or end all fracking, shale and ocean extraction but allow less ecologically harmful extraction to take place if new deposits are found away from protected land. Somehow, in some effective, intelligent way, we must wean ourselves from the killing pap of fossil fuel.

End private ownership of automatic assault weapons or institute age requirements and more rigorous vetting.

Institute free, universal health coverage for all and eliminate all health insurance. (Yes, horror of horrors, nationalize our healthcare. Nearly every advanced nation on Earth has it and doctors in those countries still live well. Canada, Cuba and so many others put us to shame.)

Cut the war machine budget and allocate those funds to improving education, infrastructure and social services. Military spending should be twenty percent of our total discretionary budget, not over half. We could cut it to fifty percent the first year, down from about fifty-four, then five percent each year till it becomes a sane, reasonable amount.

Withdraw all combat troops and support personnel from all foreign soil, abandon all bases that exist where the people and/or the country don't want them and prohibit any kind of invasion of any country, including drones, without UN sanction unless we have irrefutable evidence that we've been significantly attacked and both Houses of Congress pass a war resolution with two thirds majority. In such circumstances, of course, increased emergency funds could be allocated. It's not our job to patrol, control and rule the world.

Establish guidelines for the best free educational system in the world, the qualifications for teachers and a good living wage as their salary. Subsidize all public and state schools, from preschool to post graduate, and make them tuition free. Dissolve all debt incurred through student loans. Proclaim an end to all policies promoting the dumbing of America.

Mandate all scientific research to enter the public domain and be published freely on the Internet one year after publication date.

Institute substantial, graduated carbon and chemical pollution taxes and, perhaps, luxury item transaction taxes and the best, most equitable, loophole-free income tax codes our nation has ever had and strengthen the laws against evasion and havens.

And our Fourth Amendment rights have all but been stripped away by our drug law enforcing police state, our corrupt Supreme Court and our pandemic electronic surveillance so they need to be reinforced, as well.

And, if it were up to me, mandate meditation instruction at every level of our educational system beginning in third grade. All different kinds could be taught, both religious and secular, and students could choose any or none to practice on their own time, depending on their readiness and predilection. But at least they'd get regular tastes of what could truly help us all the most and bring those deeper, more peaceful, loving and beautiful energies into their school environments.

I'd also ban giant feed lots and the inhumane treatment of our feed animals and issue apologies to every nation we have ever in some way screwed.

Perhaps we could also address our immigration policies or whatever else might arise out of the brilliant, collective mind of some of the best of our nation.

I know this sounds completely wild, radical and pie-in-the-sky, but it ain't necessarily so. Think of it, not really a runaway convention or a stupid one, a Home Run Convention, an enlightened one with expert minds crafting the changes we so desperately need, a knock-it-out-of-the-park, giant leap forward for the people of America and for the world we live in.

Yes, I'll say it, a New American Revolution, peaceful, constitutional and brilliant, not against the King of England, but against the Kings of Commerce who rule us and our world far more autocratically, pervasively and harshly than George ever could.

A True American Revolution, of, by and for the people.

A New American Evolution brought about by us.

For if not us, who? Certainly not our politicians, courts or President.

And if not now, when? When it's too late? It nearly is.

We have reached the point where radical reform is truly necessary or, more fundamentally, what MLK so clearly saw and repeatedly expressed towards the end of his life and we haven't begun to conceive of:

"A radical revolution of values"

"A radical redistribution of economic and political power"

"A radical restructuring of the architecture of American society"

So as to "begin the shift from a thing-oriented society to a person-oriented society."

And, I would say, from a money-oriented to a health-and-well-being-oriented society or from an oligarch-ordered to a people-and-nature-ordered society.

We could make a huge beginning if we could convince thirty-four states to have a convention in the first place, if we were intelligent enough to propose a whole slate of world-improving amendments and if thirty-eight states were intelligent enough to ratify some or most of them.

I know all this is a big IF, but what other recourse is there at this point in the disintegration of our world? We just might pull it off.

Every state could examine each amendment separately and decide whether to ratify or not. And if any, like Prohibition, were passed but misguided, it could be repealed.

It's time for us to move beyond allowing our fear to rule us.

It's time for us to break out of our box.

For the sad truth is that we the sheeple, more and more, have become owned by the system.

We are in bondage, rats in the maze constructed by the Lords of Money.

We are all in a prison of sorts.

Life doesn't have to be this difficult.

It is not meant to be.

When the great bulk of power and wealth is amassed and held by the very few, it sucks much of the life, freedom, dignity and opportunity out of the hands of the many.

We become drones on a treadmill to continue feeding their money machine.

It's those in power who have corralled us into a form of slavery and have sown the fear of the runaway convention in us.

They don't want us running away from them.

It's those in power who have dictated that so many don't deserve a living wage, that unions must be weak, that only the lucky, money-oriented, select few deserve decent, graceful lives.

They have always feared us.

They have always sought to control us.

And they have succeeded almost utterly, now nearly to the

point of taking us all down with them.

The survival of our food supply, our oceans, ourselves and our planet really is at stake.

God's Earth does not belong to the moneyed.

She belongs to all of us.

She belongs to herself, God and future generations.

We have no right to be her decimators.

Let us throw off this yoke.

Our Home of the Brave is not as free or courageous as we would like to believe.

We have given away our power.

Let us reclaim it.

Our wise forefathers wrote Article V into our Constitution to give us a way to set things right.

Let us use it.

Let us have the second Constitutional Convention in the history of our nation.

Let us take back our country and our world.

Let us learn to think and grow strong.

It is time. It is needed. It is nearly the only thing left to us, the only thing big enough to turn our nation.

And what a thing if we did!

I am not an expert at any of these things. We really would have to find the best, ethical minds we could and get their input in certain areas.

The whole world, economic, money flow issue is monumental.

But it's clearly been hijacked. And I know we could sort it out, dismantle certain things, institute others and redress the manipulated imbalance in reasonable, just ways that won't punish or destroy business or motivation—set things right so that taxes and money flow would have a chance to be more sensibly and equitably managed without overcompensating.

And if a business entity gambles away its money, it should go down the tubes, not be bailed out by the rest of us. And if there was wrongdoing, the perpetrators should be punished no matter how elevated their wealth status is.

So maybe we need an amendment about these things, too.

Let's get real.

Things have gotten completely out of control.

We could do this.

Let honesty, decency, integrity and intelligence prevail.

All along, I have been optimistic.

Because all along I have believed that we truly are getting to the point of making an evolutionary leap.

And all along I have continued to believe in our basic decency.

Perhaps I am wrong.

Perhaps I'm just dreaming.

Perhaps the human race has become a failed experiment.

And this is yet another world that its inhabitants will destroy.

Forgive me, I do believe it has happened elsewhere and that some of us were involved.

In our nearly infinite omniverse, so many things have happened in so very many places.

Or perhaps we won't destroy ourselves but will limp along as we have with little improvement or degradation or continued slight improvement, which I do believe has been occurring.

But I don't think so.

We've gone beyond that.

We're looking at an upward or downward plunge.

So let's join hands, shall we?

Let's do what we can.

Let's help Wolf-PAC or the cause of our choosing.

Let's transcend and incorporate Wolf-PAC and resolve to have our multi-amendment convention.

Let's retake our very lives.

We could transform our world if enough of us could wrap our heads around it.

Don't just skim and dismiss this.

Reread it a few times.

Come up with your own solutions.

Think of what we could do with determined will.
I believe in you.
I hope it's justified.

11 DO IT YOURSELFISM

Electing officials to do it for us is obviously not working.

We're going to have to do it ourselves.

Naomi Klein and her husband got sixty people together in Canada to brainstorm what was needed and The Leap was born. Now it's growing in leaps and bounds.

Cenk Uygur, a Turkish-American conservative-turned-progressive commentator, got sick of seeing our politicians and institutions bought with corrupt money and Wolf-PAC was born. Now five states have passed the resolution with more forthcoming.

Paul Hawken, ever the enlightened activist, got serious about climate disruption and spearheaded research, put it together in a book and devised a plan called Project Drawdown to do something about it.

This is from their website.

Our organization did not make or devise the plan—we found the plan because it already exists. We gathered a qualified and diverse group of researchers from around the world to identify, research, and model the 100 most substantive, existing solutions to address climate change. What was uncovered is a path forward that can roll back global warming within thirty years. It shows that humanity has the means at hand. Nothing new needs to be invented. The solutions are in place and in action. Our work is to accelerate the knowledge and growth of what is possible. We chose the name Drawdown because if we do not name the goal, we are unlikely to achieve it.

Drawdown meetings are popping up around the country and probably around the world.

They and Northwest Earth Institute then held an Eco-Challenge.

People are digging in to do what they can.

Newer, better, more profound and potentially effective things are afoot.

Something is bubbling up within the human race.

The beginnings of the real transition from the old paradigm to the new.

We must start doing everything we can.

In one way or another, all of us can do something.

There really is something good germinating within us.

The apathetic are starting to galvanize.

An invigorated citizenry could work wonders.

Instead of focusing on how terrible things are and how worthless 'they' all are, it's time to get up and act.

There are so many groups and efforts that have been doing such wonderful work for so long, though many have become money makers for their own elite.

But there's new effort materializing that has even greater potential for bringing about the real change we so greatly need, like the three above, Represent.Us, Regeneration International, the Unrig the System Summit, The People's Summit and what Katie Fahey is doing with Voters Not Politicians. And I'm sure there are more.

Nearly all our recent leaders have been such disappointments, as presidents and congressmen so often are.

We can no longer afford to look to others, no matter what position they might hold.

There are some wonderful people out there running for office.

Bernie Sanders' Our Revolution is doing what it can to

support them.

Others are, too.

By all means, if we can, let's also rise up and vote the corrupt out of office.

But the way real change is going to happen is by our bringing it about ourselves.

We must lead by example.

We can you know.

You are far more powerful than you realize.

And the inner work is a crucial part of preparing the ground for it to manifest in our troubled world.

If you haven't done much, begin.

But enough of us have been for long enough.

Outer action is now necessary to save our world.

The need is great.

The solutions are there.

People are starting to come forward.

It will take massive effort.

More and more of us will be needed.

I do believe that, at some point, something will arise that all the disparate, truly forward moving movements, organizations, projects and people will be able to coalesce around.

When that happens, we will become unstoppable.

Who, what or how that will be, I do not know, though a Constitutional Convention could very well form the core of the snowball.

If we do manage to have it, David Johnson, The Leap, Drawdown, Wolf-PAC and TimesUp people, Michelle Alexander, Bernie Sanders, Al Gore, Noam Chomsky and all the rest of the best we can find should be there, including, of course, a few of our highest integrity, Constitutional legal minds (Laurence Tribe?).

But however things unfold, it's time to get busy.

Everything for the good we now do will bear fruit and build the foundation.

Find a venue that taps into your passion.

Pick an effort already underway.
Start your own.
Get involved to whatever degree is right for you.
Begin the process and let it unfold.
You can help.
We need as many as possible.
It's time.

12 BURSTING THE BUBBLE

I have many beliefs that few share.

In this book, I have written more of the world than I usually do.

Healing, energy and the spiritual realms are usually what call me more.

So at the risk of nullifying all I have written, I would like to burst the boundaries.

As I've stated, I believe we are eternal, multidimensional beings.

Let me amplify.

The most important thing about our lives is how much we learn and evolve as a soul, as a spiritual, cognitive, loving being.

Nothing else comes close.

We are all on the journey.

God, the world or we ourselves will give us diseases, death or all kinds of tribulations if that is what will most help us learn and evolve. I learned a tremendous amount from the metastasized cancer that hit my eighteen-year-old body.

I learned a tremendous amount from my own struggles with drugs, depression, mental illness and psychotic episodes.

We have eternity, though not the eternity to burn in hell, the comic book version created by the venal, third-chakra church father liars to consolidate their control on the souls of others. No God would delight in eternal torture.

We have one in which to evolve into the highest manifestation of our being.

So, even if we destroy our world, it's not over for any of us.

We go elsewhere to learn more and do better.

The spirit continues in any of a hundred trillion places.

But I also believe that, in our growth, we are meant to do as much good as we can.

Our highest essence is love, forgiveness, acceptance and benevolence.

We are part of the evolutionary stream of all things. The more we support that and create benefit, the better it is for our soul's journey.

So I believe in each of us doing what we can to make this world a better place for ourselves, our loved ones and all who share this world with us, animal, vegetable, mineral and human.

And, of course, for all those who will come into the world that we have made.

We really are meant to be caretakers, lovers, supporters.

We are meant to grow to encompass all.

We are the keepers of everything.

This divine impulse of benevolence may look very different to each of us when applied to worldly solutions, but I believe it does exist in us all.

I also believe that life, people and the world can greatly distort or nearly expunge it.

And that now, in the death throes of the five-thousand-year patriarchal, third chakra age, it may seem to have nearly disappeared.

There is so much damage.

So much distortion.

So much ignorance, terror and pain.

So much horror we inflict on each other.

So much fear.

So much corruption and greed.

So much nullifying the importance and value of all else but

ourselves or our own little clique.

But this is not who we truly are.

We are truly better than that.

And there is help in healing from the things that have nearly destroyed us and that make us strike out and take all that we can, giving back as little as possible.

There is so much to remember.

Remembering who and what we truly are.

Remembering all the good there is and all that can be.

Remembering how precious life is and each one of us in it.

There is so much for us to do and become.

Or not.

13 THE AGE OF MIRACLES

You may not buy human evolution as each age climbing a chakra, but it's key.

It's important that more of us grok this.

The three lower chakras are the physical chakras, the earth chakras, the grungier chakras.

(You may not buy chakras at all, but they are energy centers in our body, each with different qualities, each successive higher one carrying the energies of higher states of consciousness and development—the root, above the perineum, the 2nd, in the womb area, the 3rd, in the center of the diaphragm, then the heart, the throat, the 'third eye' and the crown of the head. There are also sub-chakras, like the thymus, and higher and lower ones above and below the body—seven major ones in the body, twelve altogether corresponding to the twelve dimensions.)

((Do you buy that all matter is made of energy, that energy is more fundamental than matter, that energies evolve or distort to take on all kinds of different qualities? We are as much or more energy beings as we are physical. The energy part ends up being more important than the physical part. And what almost no one yet accepts is that energy, itself, is made of consciousness. The most basic holon in the universe is consciousness. It comes together to form and be contained by energy, which in turn comes together to form and be contained by matter, which in turn has nested, ever-more-complex forms, such as quark, atom, molecule, protein, cell, organ, system, body, etc.))

(((And while we're at it—all that mysterious dark energy and matter we can't see, find or account for? Nothing mysterious about it. It's not that it's dark. It's too light, subtle or amorphous, too celestially divine, for us or our instruments to as yet detect, though many humans have caught glimpses— the higher vibrational waves, particles and energies that dwell in and form the things and beings of the higher dimensions of which there are three times as many as the three we are used to and which end up being far more significantly substantial than the crude, dense matter of which we are made. And there are other remote universes and contiguous parallel ones that comprise our extraordinary omniverse and exert their influence, as well.)))

Most of us have evolved through the first two chakras and are living the third, though there are many groups and individuals still living the first or second and, likewise, many living the higher ones. But the great bulk of the human race, the collective as a whole, is unconsciously contemplating the leap from the third to the fourth and fifth. And there are developmental sub-levels within each chakra stage.

The heart is the first higher chakra and the mediator between the physical and the spiritual. It partakes of many of the higher qualities.

The throat is the will and bringing our essence, to whatever degree it has evolved, into the world.

The leap from the physical chakras to the higher is a greater one than the leap from the first to the second or the second to the third and, in making it, evolution speeds up to more thoroughly encompass two chakras instead of only one—three if you count the thymus sub-chakra.

In some ways, each of the successive lower chakra ages was worse than the last, in some ways better.

In our collective consciousness, the human race

remembers the far distant past as a golden age.

There are reasons for this.

There are grand cycles, which we won't get into here. But just as the oceanic awareness of oneness is experienced by the infant, the people of the first chakra age knew an elemental form of oneness that bonded them with all things in the natural world, the world, itself, the stars and the cosmos.

They knew the eternal, universal unity that we have lost.

They were more in tune with everything than we have been since and could cognize truths and wisdom that diminished when the first separation took place as the species evolved to second chakra functioning.

That's why they were able to build Newgrange, Stonehenge and so many astronomical predictors around the world that we still marvel at.

Also, there was far more harmony between the sexes and ages, a simple acceptance, understanding and honoring of each person's skills, abilities and place, and of their souls, strengths and weaknesses.

And the dominant, male hunter/protectors honored and nurtured the women and children far more than abused them, at least the ones in their own tribe.

And just so, the second chakra age was far more harmonious, nurturing and understanding, far less violent and dominant than our third chakra age.

And now, at the end of this age, we are seeing the worst of us come to the forefront to be embraced as not only acceptable but as our chosen leaders.

All of this has the potential to change fairly quickly.

While our current patriarchal men and women still deride the bleeding hearts, deep down we all really know that the heart can be wiser than the head or the separatist, materialistic, Machiavellian third chakra, in which the more I win and the more you lose, the better.

With an activated throat chakra, we have the great potential of more thoroughly accessing our higher, divine will and wisdom. In living from these higher chakras, when you lose, no matter where you may be on the planet, I lose, as well. We all know that we can both win, even if there is some seeming sacrifice.

There are such things as mutually beneficial, the common good, collaboration instead of competition and conquest.

Developmental evolution is a process of ever greater expansion and acceptance.

Most of us are 'for' ourselves, our friends and our families, our own loved ones and our group—those we identify with. This can also expand to our own race, country, religious group, political party, etc.

Evolution takes a giant leap when we learn to be for 'others' as well, when we start to realize we're all here on spaceship Earth together, when it begins to penetrate that it's all of us who will float or drown, that there are no 'others,' that you're really just a different version of me at a different or similar stage of evolution or in different or similar skin, that loving thy neighbor as thyself really does mean loving thy neighbor as thyself because he or she ultimately is thyself and that everyone on planet Earth is now your neighbor.

This last can be a terrifying thought for many but, more and more, it's simply true. The modern world is throwing us all together and making us all very close neighbors.

Instead of trying to separate and isolate ourselves, to strengthen the barriers and build walls, to protect ourselves by diminishing, hating or destroying the enemy, instead of fighting each other, our sense of self expands to include the other and, wonder of wonders, the enemy disappears and becomes an extended, greater part of ourselves. We want to help them instead of destroy them, help them survive, thrive and grow in their own inner and outer development.

We're all evolving together, though at different rates and at different stages.

But the more that each lonely person evolves, the better it is for everyone.

In whatever way we help ourselves or anyone else, we help everyone.

The deeper acceptance of this greater heartedness is world changing.

Of course many don't want our help and don't think they need it, but that's beside the point.

As more individuals grow into the wisdom of the greater good or ending the fight or turquoise life[1], we get closer and closer to making the leap and seeing it manifest in the world we live in.

If we don't destroy ourselves, if we succeed in navigating the birthing transition from gut dominance to heart and throat dominance, we have the potential of seeing a truly transformed world—an Age of Miracles. Because what we see will look like miracles compared to what we've been living till now.

This is potentially a very exciting time or an increasingly disastrous one.

I believe that many civilizations in our nearly infinite, eternal omniverse have destroyed themselves and their worlds or other civilizations at this juncture, when their technologies have evolved to the point where they could and their internal, psychological, spiritual evolution was stuck in third chakra functioning, just as many individuals commit suicide while others murder.

We have done this before.

We have learned.

It's time to bring it all together.

In one way, it's about priorities.

What, truly, is important?

Money and power at the cost of all else?

That's what's killing us.

Beauty, grace, quality of life, quality of environment, fairness, equity, loving support, tolerance, inclusiveness, cleaning up our mess, benevolent activism?

You may sneer.

All bleeding-heart qualities.

But that's what will save us.

And you.

You do have an eternal soul and these qualities are its

highest currency—money in the bank of your evolution.

And what will we see if our world starts being transformed by these things?

A renaissance world that'll put all the smaller renaissances to shame.

They foreshadowed our potential.

Geniuses popping up everywhere instead of only a handful throughout history.

An explosion in wisdom, art, freedom and science.

Unprecedented worldwide collaboration.

Great numbers of us thriving and helping others thrive, living well instead of obscenely, generating joyous abundance instead of bloat and lack.

More true compatibles more easily finding each other.

A lot more soul mingling and genuine love and a lot less groping.

Fewer and fewer murdering berserkers.

Fewer and fewer religious fanatics.

Who knows?

Let's see!

It's time to do more than dream.

We must take our world back.

We must change the unchangeable.[2]

14 THE MIRACLES BEGIN

I have always felt like a human bellwether, riding the crest of the rock and roll, drug, sexual and spiritual revolutions.

Now we're at the cusp of the Miracle Revolution.

Or we're not.

We're at the cusp of a huge downward spiral that could very well end in our extinction.

So I can't help believe[3] that if miracles start happening for me, they will also start in the world and for others.

I am seeing the beginnings of these miracles in The Leap, Wolf-PAC, Project Drawdown, BEAM and the Cognition Enhancer, in Aaron Swartz before his untimely death, in Michelle Alexander exposing what has been massively hidden before our eyes, in #MeToo, #TimesUp and the women's marches, in #MarchforOurLives, the school walkouts and #Enough—Enough of all of the B.S. Everywhere—and in the proliferating teachers' strikes, which the press barely reports.

But am I just reading in, indulging in wishful thinking?

Good things are always happening here and there, are they not?

Are these harbingers of a revolution or is nothing really changing?

Are we nearly ripe? For ripeness is all. Or are we just going from green to rot?

For me, this book is a miracle. My previous have been written in isolation, self-published and, whether I tried to promote them or not, hardly read, with little or no outer connection to the world or attendant gifts of synchronicity with the exception of my play, which is another story altogether.

But knowledge of the above 'miracles' came to me through synchronicity and other gifts around the book have similarly appeared.

It is more deeply embedded in the world and supported by it than my previous efforts.

If I'm able to truly get it published and it reaches any kind of significant number, it will certainly be a personal miracle, but it will also hearten me greatly about our future as a species.

I have always felt that I am destined to make an impact in the world, to help a large number of people and to help the world evolve.

This has clearly been fed and overblown by my ego, my biochemical challenges, my grandiosity and my megalomania.

And it's never happened, or only briefly on a smaller scale.

But I also can't help but hope that there is still truth in it.

I have been terrified of success. As a very young child, I made an unconscious vow to avoid it at all costs because I didn't want to be like my father. This also inhibited my ability to truly love and feel good about myself.

If I haven't fulfilled my mission, my destiny, the purpose of my being, then I have failed. I'm no good. I'm unworthy of love. (Just as a one-year-old, how could I not interpret my mother's cutting me off, my father's newly begun, frequent, vicious attacks and my being shut out of the family circle of love as irrefutable proof I was something monstrous, I had done some terrible, unforgivable wrong even though, try as I might, I couldn't comprehend what it was?)

These are the kinds of double, triple and quadruple binds the world can deliver or we can tie our own lives up with.

The good news is that the writing of this book and the synchronicity around it have helped me break through all this more than ever, though I've been chipping away at it all my life.

So whether I'm able to secure a real publishing deal or whether or not more than a few read this, I have just broken through to a better, deeper quantum level of love, acceptance and being.

And I let it all go while continuing to do what I can.

So it has wrought these miracles in my life, let alone the great fulfilment of writing and improving it.

But let's put me aside, though the following would seem the opposite.

Because it's only when we're truly able to step aside and become the hollow reed that we open the door for real outer miracles to come forth, which I was especially supported in doing with the thousand or so people I worked with during my thirteen-months in South Africa and Botswana. (See the far too many testimonials on my website.)

And, of course, doing one's inner work is the necessary opposite of this. We must, by definition, focus deeply within ourselves to effect it.

So may the miracles proliferate, thick and fast.

Why have I written this?

What do I hope to achieve?

As I've repeated, we need to rethink our world.

We need a vision of the future.

We need to grok our own growth processes and a new way forward of living and being.

We need a more profound appreciation of our condition and its cure.

But we also need more of us to join in, on every level, as many as possible, and do the inner and outer work.

As Paul Hawken says, we need a narrative.

Or, as I would say, we need our context.

A deeper understanding.

A cohesive dream.

A vision of possibilities.

A reminder of our higher Realities.

We need to make it explicit, spell it out, make it obvious, have it crystalize in our consciousness.

Then we have to get off our duff and do something about it.

We all have smaller and greater selves, one for each chakra.

We often live the smaller but sometimes we rise up to live the greater.

We need to find our better selves in a mass rising.

This is yet another one of my attempts to contribute.

If you want to help yourself, your loved ones and the world, read *End the Fight*, *What We Can Do* and *The Love and Forgiveness Meditation* and put their contents into practice.

If you want to know more about me, read *I Love You and Forgive You*.

If you want to expand your fun, sex and fantasy life, read *The Miracle Revolution*.

And if you profoundly feel the latter was written for you and you want to help me live, be and do my work, don't hesitate to let me know.

But most importantly, get proactive.

Find a venue to support and work through that can help our world.

Or, if you're not quite ready for that, do the inner work.

Just incorporating the Love and Forgiveness Meditation (L&F) or another deep, mostly effortless one into your daily routine and doing it every day would do more to make our world healthier than you know.

We're all connected.

No man is an island.

If all of Earth's water were to disappear, there would be one continuous landmass, one big chunk of soil, sand, silt and rock, one ocean-less bottom.

Just like that, at our depths, we're all one seething lump of vibration, energy, thoughts, emotions, despair, hopes and dreams.

One morphic energy field without skin color, nationality, gender or religion.

Each person has an effect.

We each radiate all the time, transmit, uplift or depress this collective.

No one is perfectly neutral.

As I write this our chosen leader, the President of the United States, just dismissed a continent of shithole nations, Mother Africa, our human birthplace, where he, himself, and we all originated, where I had some of my most glorious experiences because it's so vibrant, sustaining and energetically powerful. If it weren't so sad it would be funny. But he's already dismissed half the human race, its women, and almost everyone else besides himself, his family and a small, admired coterie of people just like him, the epitome of third and first chakra functioning.

We are now truly pitiful, the most foolish of petulant babies in the greatest need of love and a spanking, though this is a classic case of projection—a shithole president in denial of and unable to own and perceive his own shithole tendencies, casting them out as aspersions against countries, a continent and a race of others to give himself a false sense of superiority and relief. We can only spank ourselves by feeling our shame and loving ourselves and vowing to pull ourselves out of this shithole we have sunk ourselves into and do better.

(And what a sweet, beautiful organ the anus actually is. So much of all this really does come down to our own, dysfunctional self-loathing, having been inculcated with visceral fear and disgust towards our own souls and intimate bodily functions, which, as infants, we couldn't differentiate. So we carry this self-hatred throughout our lives and try to free ourselves of it by projecting it onto others. And what a wonderful model our president is for illustrating these salient points!)

On March 14, 2018, tens of thousands of students left their classes to protest school shootings and the United Nations Sustainable Development Solutions Network issued its World Happiness Report 2018.

Think there could be a connection between national health and happiness and mass murders? Think the children might feel it more than the adults?

Think these two things happening on the same day was purely coincidental?

In my world, this was subtle, mysterious divine orchestration, a wink from God.

"Hello, are you there? Time to wake up a little more. Look to your children. Look to yourselves. Are you shepherds or thieves? Do you nurture or diminish? Come home to your divine wisdom."

Everything is either intelligent or stupid, in accord with wisdom, benevolence and integrity or opposed to it.

We are too enamored of greed, violence and stupidity.

They are opposed to our God Selves.

America dropped four points to become eighteenth on the happiness list, significantly below most wealthy countries. Finland, Norway, Denmark, Iceland, Switzerland, the Netherlands, Canada, New Zealand, Sweden and Australia are the top ten.

While we still have more money than most, our social measures suck. Those countries where people are happiest have social democracies where the governments take good care of their citizens instead of squeezing them, undermining them and setting things up to incarcerate and marginalize as many of them as possible.

Our life expectancy and confidence in our government are decreasing and our drug dependency, suicides rates, corruption, mass shootings and inequality are increasing. We are under significant stress as we continue to misbehave at home and abroad.

Let's do something about it.

In a very primeval way, we are all responsible for everything. We all contain everything. There is nothing out there that is not within. We only become mature by becoming this responsibility and totality to whatever degree we can.

For we could also be the train that can.
There's New York City.
The lowest crime rate since the 50s.
This is a collective phenomenon.
Everything is a collective phenomenon.
There are individual actions.
But even these are influenced by collective pressures.
And this is indicative, hopeful, a hint of what's to come if we can get there, something we can be heartened by and proud of.

(New York and California are ahead of the curve. What a shame if they were to be swallowed by the sea, though some folks might like that idea.)

((And is everything I write nothing but me thinking to myself, my own form of auto-confirmation, my compensatory, mental masturbation? Yes and no, both and neither, more than both and less than neither, and something more.))

We could make a wonderful world.
Help us heal it.
Help us rebirth it.
Help us make it stronger, more balanced and more equitable.
Help us re-sanctify it.
We need to help each other.
We have degraded every aspect of our existence.
We pay lip service to 'under God,' but our actions belie it.
Instead of using it to inspire us to divine behavior, we use it as license to dominate.
Our hierarchy of values is upside down and inside out.
It now puts life in jeopardy.
We must re-inform our behavior towards everything with the highest integrity.
We must return to truth and make it paramount.
As many of us as possible must come to deeper love and understanding.
In one way, the pagans were right.

Everything is sacred.

Sacredness is omnipresently inherent.

Or can be if you decide to live that way.

Everything is precious.

Including you.

Spirit is more important than money.

Heart, the content of character, benevolence is more important than skin color, fame or power-in-the-world.

Thin, small spirits rule our world.

Men with dollar signs for eyes, cash registers for hearts.

Men who have perennially been screwing us.

Men who have been controlling, manipulating and molesting our monetary and economic policies, our war machine, our lives and the sanctity, health and well-being of Mother Earth.

Soulless machines (though not really).

Sick, greedy, ignorant throwbacks.

Men who can't comprehend so don't give a hoot about the greater good of life, the world or its people.

Men who self-aggrandize to the detriment of all.

Men who fight life, themselves and everyone and everything around them.

Men of third chakra evolution—the old, dying, killing paradigm.

We can have compassion for them.

(They, too, can be redeemed.)

We can know that we contain them within us.

But we must find them, call them out and stop them.

Not only the obvious public figureheads, but the Board members, CEOs and owners of the worst polluting corporations, the masters of war, money and the desecration of food, the Wizards of Oz behind their curtains and the arcane levers they have been pulling to control and amass the flow of wealth and our world economies.[4]

Beware.

Wake up.

The lionhearts are coming.

YOUR TIME IS UP!

There have always been those behind and ahead of their time.
But the future is ours.
If we can secure it.
We have great inner and outer work to do.
Let's begin.
Let's join those who have begun.
And the innumerable who have given their lives.
Let's fulfill their work and sacrifice.
Let's do more.
Do what you can.
The more you do on your own or the world's highest behalf, the more you help.
Truly.
You make a difference.
So make the best one you can.
If you've been doing the outer, activist work, add the inner healing/spiritual, the developmental, the evolutional, the meditational, the difficult, painful shadow work—as Wilber so pithily puts it, the Show Up, Grow Up, Wake Up and Clean Up work.[5]
So many of us have been doing it so deeply for so long that it will go more quickly and easily for those who now seriously come to it.
If this is what you've been doing, add the activist.
We now need to dig in to help save the life of our world and it will invigorate you in wonderful ways to get busy on the world's behalf.
If you've been doing neither, add one or both.
If both, God bless you, keep on. If we're lucky, you'll soon see an influx of fresh, new help.
I expect to see this greater expansion and unification of our activist and spiritual nations.
A new resurgence of the truly good.
The rise of the feminine and the turquoise people after five thousand years of crude, third chakra, masculine

dominance.

The balance and unification of the masculine and feminine, the spiritual and material.

The burgeoning of the Rainbow World so many of us have seen from the mountaintop.

The flowering of our highest, bestest, rightest stuff.

The Great Leap.

The Miracle Revolution.

The Promised Land.

The reassertion of our Divine Blueprint.

The inception of our Rise after eons of living our Fall.

The First Age of the Higher Chakras.

The New American Evolution.

The higher, divine potential that many peoples and cultures have known to somewhere exist so have mythically and presciently projected onto some hypothetical locale as Shambhala, Hyperborea and so many others, but which, in reality, resides inherently within each and every one of us as latent, quiescent potency, exists eternally in the highest dimensions, did somewhat develop, in actuality, in little pockets here and there on Earth, most notably in the Himalayas, and could become more collectively forthcoming worldwide than it ever has been in the history of mankind if we don't self-destruct.

Our inner divine spark or field and the higher-dimensional True Christ Realm, Kingdom of Heaven, Field of All Possibilities, which most of us have sometime experienced or lived, are one.

It is not small or mean. It does not despise. It does not lust to squeeze the life out of others, for it sees no 'other.' It is all-encompassing and inclusive and seeks to love, nourish and support all that is. It takes delight in seeing each and every flower shine forth in all its glory.

We see it every day but we have mostly lost sight of it.

More and more, it could rule our world.

Chaitanya.

All the gods, saints, masters and angels.

In the name of Jesus, Muhammed, Kuan Yin and Kali.

Republican and Democrat.

And the One God above in all Her glory and with all His manifestations.

Let's invoke ourselves and all the help we can get.

Let's move beyond jealous, fighting, hating Gods and come together.

Things could become glorious.

Get on board.

Let's do it.

Let's evolve, survive and thrive.

We inhabit an amazing, precious world.

And we desecrate it.

Our incomprehensibly vast, magnificent universe came forth from a point, one nearly infinitely hot, small dot. It, in turn, came forth from the Great, Eternal Everything/Nothing, which always was, is and will be.

You came forth from one tiny sperm, a dot with a tail, and a larger egg, like a tiny sun or planet, both jam-packed with living, binding programming in the form of long strands of mind-bogglingly complex DNA coded in four molecules.

Imagine the programming in the infinitely smaller universe singularity!

If these are not Miracles, what are?

Someday, perhaps, we'll wise up and begin to do them justice.

Let's wise up now and do what we can to turn the coming storm, flood and fire.

[1]My dear architect friend, Aaron Bohrer, gave me Ken Wilber's *Trump and a Post-Truth World* after completing this book but early on in the editing stages. He had also given me *A Brief History of Everything* a long time ago, but Ken's agonizingly academic style stopped me dead in my tracks. But I did read his Trump book and am glad I did. It crystalized a number of things for me and gave me some verbiage, which led to some additions to chapters three and thirteen. I prefer chakra wisdom, which he assiduously avoids, but we're very much on the same page and he's done some great work in laying out holons, the integral nature of developmental levels, which he denotes by colors—turquoise being the highest he mentions in the book—and quadrants of existence.

[2]Ralph Abernathy via dear, astonishing Maya Angelou, *The Heart of a Woman*, 1981, p. 54. (Not astonishingly wry, decent, poetically articulate and clear 'for a black woman,' but for anyone, man, woman, white, black or green, just as MLK was not only, as she wrote on the next page, "the best we (the blacks) had," but whose turquoise splendor eclipsed that of pretty much everyone else on Earth at the time or since. There is a kind of valid elitism whereby we allow ourselves to admire and admit the best in us and the best we can become instead of hating and killing it and we can acknowledge and allow the worst in us to just flow through and subside without acting out, hating or misguidedly trying to kill it. And for those who might be helped by this, impulses may arise within us not only from our own small selves but from others or the collective, as well.)

[3]I've alluded to belief a lot in this book. I'd like to say something more about it. There are beliefs and facts. There is truth and untruth. My height can be measured. If I'm six feet tall, that's a fact. I may believe I'm eight feet and tell everyone so but that doesn't make it true. When beliefs deny facts, they become delusional. 1st chakra life is dominated by magic. If I draw something on my cave wall and invest it with fervor, the object will come to me. The 2nd chakra is myth-based. I can't

make it happen but there are gods who can so I propitiate them. The 3rd chakra is belief-based. Whatever I believe or disbelieve, is inviolable. I live by my dogma. Facts don't signify. The 4th chakra is fact-based—the heart loves truth. I'm from Missouri. Show me and I'll see it's right. People living this chakra may have beliefs about things that are hard to or can't be proved or measured, but when facts come along, they are ready to change their minds. Verity and honesty count. Billions of measured atmospheric and weather data points all agree. We have altered our climate. Belief doesn't change this, one way or another. Only our actions will. (I have Ken Wilber and Paul Hawken to thank for helping me crystalize this.) As the higher chakras kick in, something new happens. The higher, eternal truths emerge. They can't be measured or proved, but discernment, direct cognition and an inner truth barometer develop that aren't infallible but that outer 'truths' can resonate with or not. A deeper, less fanatically held knowing, as opposed to false certainty, emerges. And the divine truths become more and more wonderful. So what about miracles? They can occur anywhere, anytime no matter what chakra we may be living. By definition, they are rare and unexpected. But there are things we can do to help bring them about. And they have the potential to turn into a deluge of support and synchronicity…:)

[4]Just as Paul Hawken coalesced a cadre of excellent researchers to put together the hundred best things we can now do to turn climate change around and Moira Donegan created the "Shitty Media Men" list, someone should coalesce a cadre of excellent researchers to determine the world's thousand worst thieves, polluters and money controllers—a Shitty World Dominator List—so we can expose, call them out and somehow put an end to what they are doing.

[5]Ken Wilber, *Trump and a Post-Trump World*, 2017, p. 143.

[6]An unaligned endnote. I wanted to float a phrase in the name of advancing clarity and understanding, perhaps to help us see.

In a way, higher levels of awareness, of consciousness, of heart, soul and spirit, become simpler, more real and, yes, more filled with forgiveness, acceptance, loving kindness and true, vulnerable courage as opposed to bravado, especially attack bravado. The phrase is 'living a stance.' So again, let us use our dear president as model. Ultimately, it really is noble of him to put himself so forward as he has. Everything about him shouts 'stance.' He postures, he blusters, he attacks and he holds himself a certain way, a way that, ultimately, is not simple, genuine and authentic, not real, but posed, not full, but full of himself. He thrusts his stance upon us. We have elected in our past a surprising number of men as presidents who, to me, have obviously been living a stance. Again and again, we have not been able to see through their 'glamor'—an archaic meaning of this word signifying an illusion that one is able to cast around oneself and out to others, a glowing cloak of deception. In the ancient language of India, this was referred to as the power of one's maya. And men used to pit their maya against each other. In this book I have often taken a hard-edged voice and used sarcasm as a sword to cut through ignorance and bullshit. I hope it hasn't been counterproductive. I might have been better served using a simpler, more genuine, more loving voice. Perhaps a goal for my next book. I'm acutely aware I can be snide, conceited and arrogant. Humility is one of my main lifelong lessons. And I've been living it in almost every way. But how elusive true humility really is! My dear sister recently recounted to a few of us over breakfast that her extravagant, long since deceased ex had said of me not long after meeting me, 'I love him, he's such a snot!' And how blatantly my voice can betray that. Sometimes I remind myself of William Buckley Jr. Sorry, we all have a lot to learn. But it takes one to know one. We live in a conceited nation that has caused untold misery within our borders and worldwide. We have done many wonderful things and, yes, in some ways have been 'the greatest country in the world.' But we have done so many terrible things that we refuse to own up to at the expense of so many. We must move beyond them and our deceit and corrupt practices and reclaim and act on our humility, integrity, honesty and decency towards our citizens and immigrants, other nations and Mother Earth. We must become great in our heart, soul and being and reduce our swagger. We are all on the path of evolution. We all have so very far to go. The path is long and often arduous. We all, to some degree, live both stance and genuine, simple truth. But we can, will and must become more aware, more perceptive and more knowing and understanding. We must learn to see through the spin, through the glamor, through all the pantomime. When the scales fall from our eyes, the emperor has no clothes. We have no clothes. We come up short. But now we face world resurrection or death. Which will it be? Shall we get to it?

[7]And another. We in the US have benefitted from the industrial revolution and relatively cheap fossil fuel more than any other people on Earth. Now, for our global survival, we are asking developing nations to forgo that energy. We should unite with as many developed countries as possible and massively subsidize their going straight from cow dung to renewables, just as they went from no telephones to cell phones. And we should subsidize their rejuvenated agriculture and education as well as the renewal of our own. It would not only help save our lives and world but would be payback for all we have stolen from the weak and poor.

Thanks to Richard Jennings for turning me on to The Leap,
BEAM and Drawdown, John Wantz for turning me on to
Wolf-PAC, Shannon Young White for soul mingling and
helping me soften the book's induction and Maharishi
Mahesh Yogi, Leslie Temple-Thurston and L&F for helping
me more thoroughly know and awaken
my selves and chakras.

I write books, plays and songs, do healing work
and live in Santa Fe.
Helping others meet and process their trauma
is some of my most important work.
I also do Highest Dimensional Energy Healing (HDEH) and
call in the devas and light energies to help with it all.
And I can teach and solidify your L&F Meditation practice.
If inspired, go to mark-landau.com, read more and email me.
There is help in our deepest, hardest, most important work.